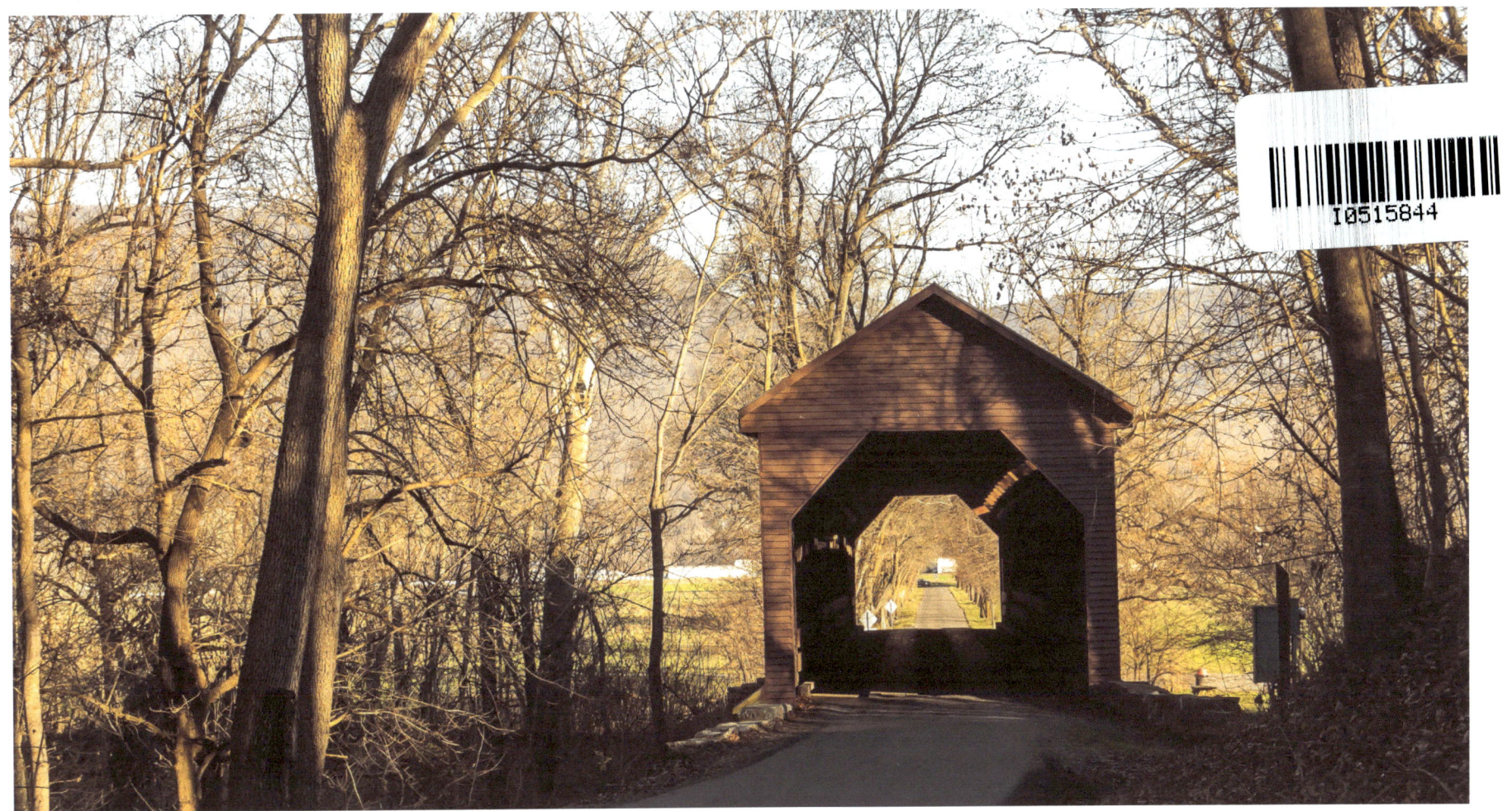

Enjoying the Beauty of Home
and
Neighboring Roundabouts

Shirley Nan Washington, Ed.D.

Copyright Page

Copyright 2021 by Shirley Nan Washington

All rights reserved. This book or any portion thereof may not be reproduced or used in any manner whatsoever without the express written permission of the author or publisher.

Preface and Acknowledgments

PREFACE:

Have you ridden through Virginia's longest still-standing covered bridge with its Burr Arch Truss design, Meems Bottom Covered Bridge, in Mt. Jackson, Virginia? Have you peeked at the historic 1934 Ford Oren Firetruck at the Strasburg Fire Department or the unique classic cars at Classic Car Center Inc. in Fredericksburg, Virginia? When is the last time you traveled to Virginia's vibrant capital, Richmond, and viewed the City's rich arts and cultural scenes? Are you familiar with many of its central sight-seeing destinations, including three monuments of African Americans? Have you noticed the beautiful bluestone buildings at James Madison University and Virginia Union University? Have you caught a close-up glimpse of some of Virginia's most spectacular animals, including a donkey, gold-coated horse, swan, or peacock?

While visiting her hometown, Harrisonburg, for the Newtown Cemetery's Dedication Ceremony for listing in the National Register of Historic Places in 2015, the author discovered many of her friends, and cohorts appreciated the arts and desired to learn of additional Virginia landmarks and historical sites, including the beauty in nature.

This photographic book was created to showcase and share the amazing beauty of special animals, antiques, and the arts, captured in and nearby her hometown of Harrisonburg and its neighboring roundabouts.

ACKNOWLEDGMENTS:

The author wishes to extend her sincere appreciation to two of her Montgomery College professors in Publication Design with InDesign, and Printing Management, for their supervision and encouragement with the production and editing of this second book trilogy about home: Harry St. Ours and William J. Humphrey. In particular, her gratitude also goes to Brian Jones, Coordinator of Photography, for his photographic image review and anecdotal comments; and to the following very special and patient folks who served the role of her Photography Assistants: her sisters, Bernice, Mary Ann and Jean; her childhood buddy, Reesie; and her college friends, Raynord, Roger, and Sharon.

About the Author

The author, Shirley Nan Washington, '78 Ed.D. (UMASS), is a native of Harrisonburg, Virginia and resides in Silver Spring, Maryland. She is a retired educator and lifelong learner who is a six-time Montgomery College graduate (with honors) from the following programs of study: Paralegal Studies ('12); Criminal Justice ('13); Photography ('15); Studio Art ('18) General Art ('19) and Communication Studies ('20). Dr. Washington is a recipient of several awards, including: the Dr. Harry Harden Jr. Academic Excellence Student Medallion (2013), the Spirit of Service Medallion for Student Volunteer Service Hours (2016), and Studio Arts Award for Demonstrating Outstanding Academic Performance in the Studio Arts (2019).

Since her undergraduate studies at Virginia State University, Shirley has been actively involved in community affairs and social justice. She holds a Charter Membership in the Smithsonian's National Museum of African American History and Culture and has membership in other organizations, including: ACLU, MSEA and NEA. Her national honor society memberships include Lambda Epsilon Chi (LEX), Phi Delta Kappa, and Phi Theta Kappa. She served 13 years as Ombudsman Representative (volunteer) with the Montgomery County Long Term Care Ombudsman Program (Maryland Enhanced Certification), and she is also a former member of the Wheaton Library Advisory Committee (8 years).

Besides having a great appreciation for the visual arts: capturing photographic images of distinctive sights and sounds, creating works of art, visiting museums, etc., Shirley also enjoys playing the piano, mingling with diverse folks, and learning about drones. She has had photographic and art pieces showcased in juried student exhibitions and in the Sligo Journal.

Shirley reminisces her childhood's love of travel and fascinating art through her vividly dazzling photography. Her three colorful, photographic books showcase road trips' images from some of Virginia's finest and rarest antiques, magnificent arts, unique animals, and scenic views of the Shenandoah Valley and nearby regions. In her 184-page photographic book trilogy, Home, she revisits some of the same Virginia towns she toured as a youngster and shares findings of her picturesque journey.

Introduction

This photographic book contains 71 images of animals, antiques, and the arts which were immediately appealing, eye-catching, to the author while perusing her hometown, Harrisonburg, Virginia and traveling to its nearby roundabouts. The images are identified, to the best of her knowledge, on each page and are presented in the following sequence:

Animals   pp. 1 - 15
Antiques   pp. 16 - 39
The Arts   pp. 40 - 71

As you journey with this author, while viewing her photographs, she hopes you will find joy and splendor in the images of the unique animals, vintage objects and vehicles, and spectacular arts. Finally, she invites you to also consider visiting the places and objects she found interesting in her hometown and roundabouts. She challenges you to share your experiences through writing and publishing a book that also showcases your discovered beauty.

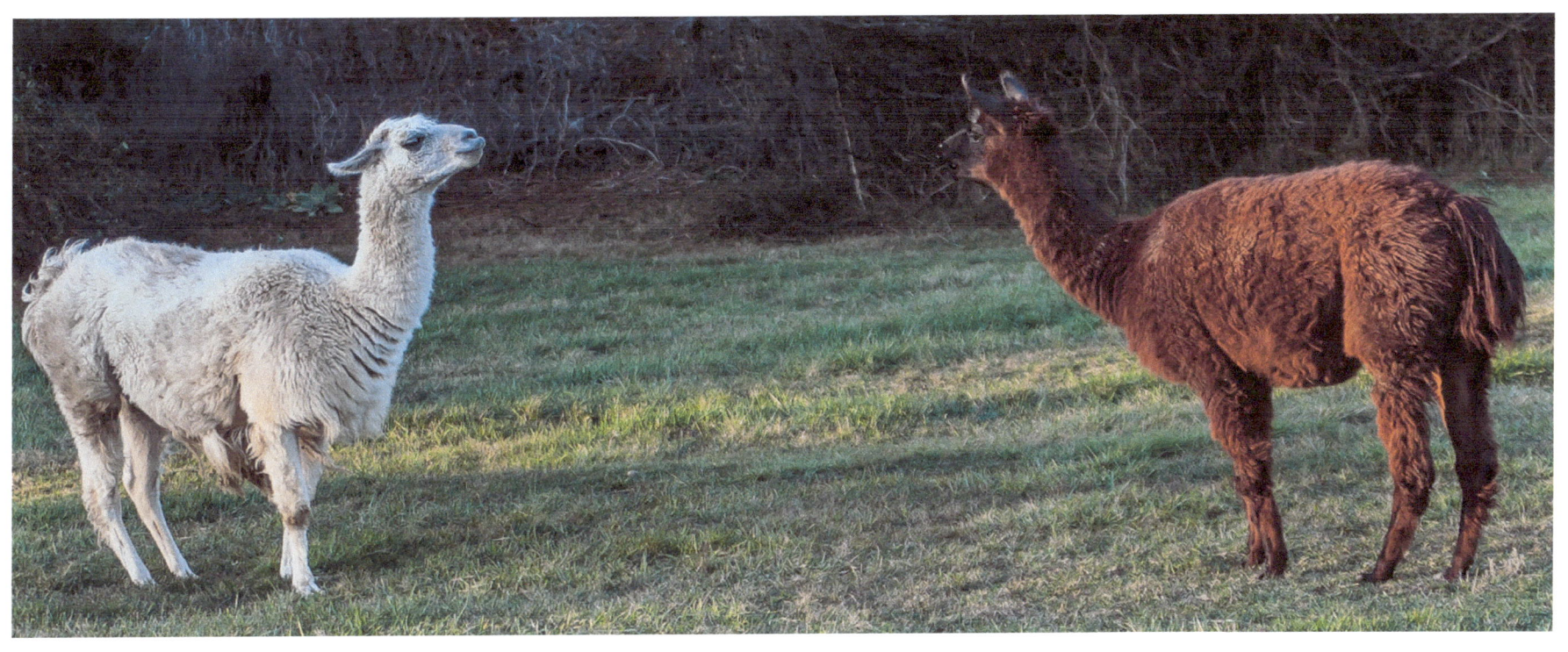

Two Alpacas "Grazing in the Grass"

A Swan Lake Beauty - Mute Swan - Smoothing Feathers

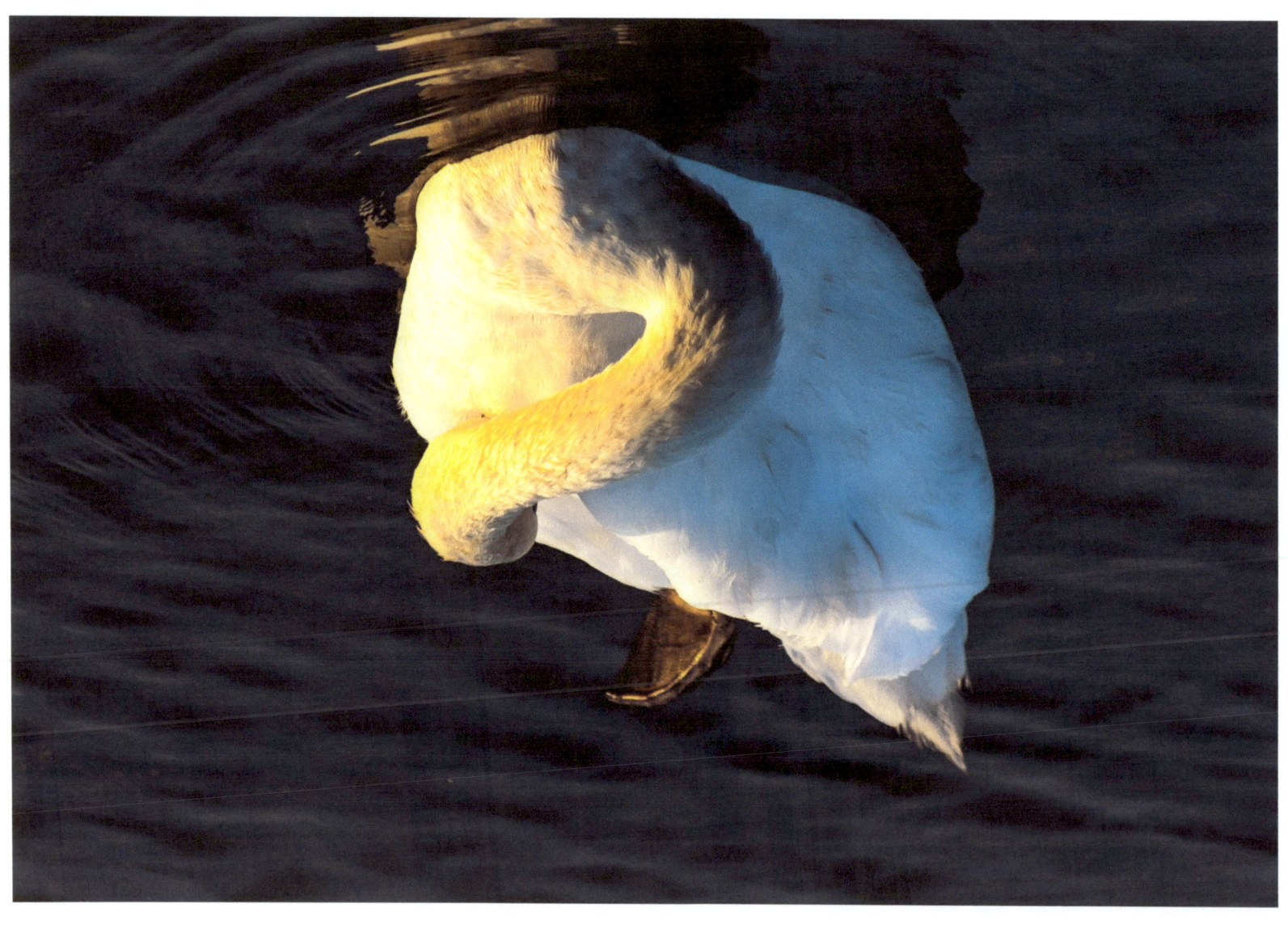

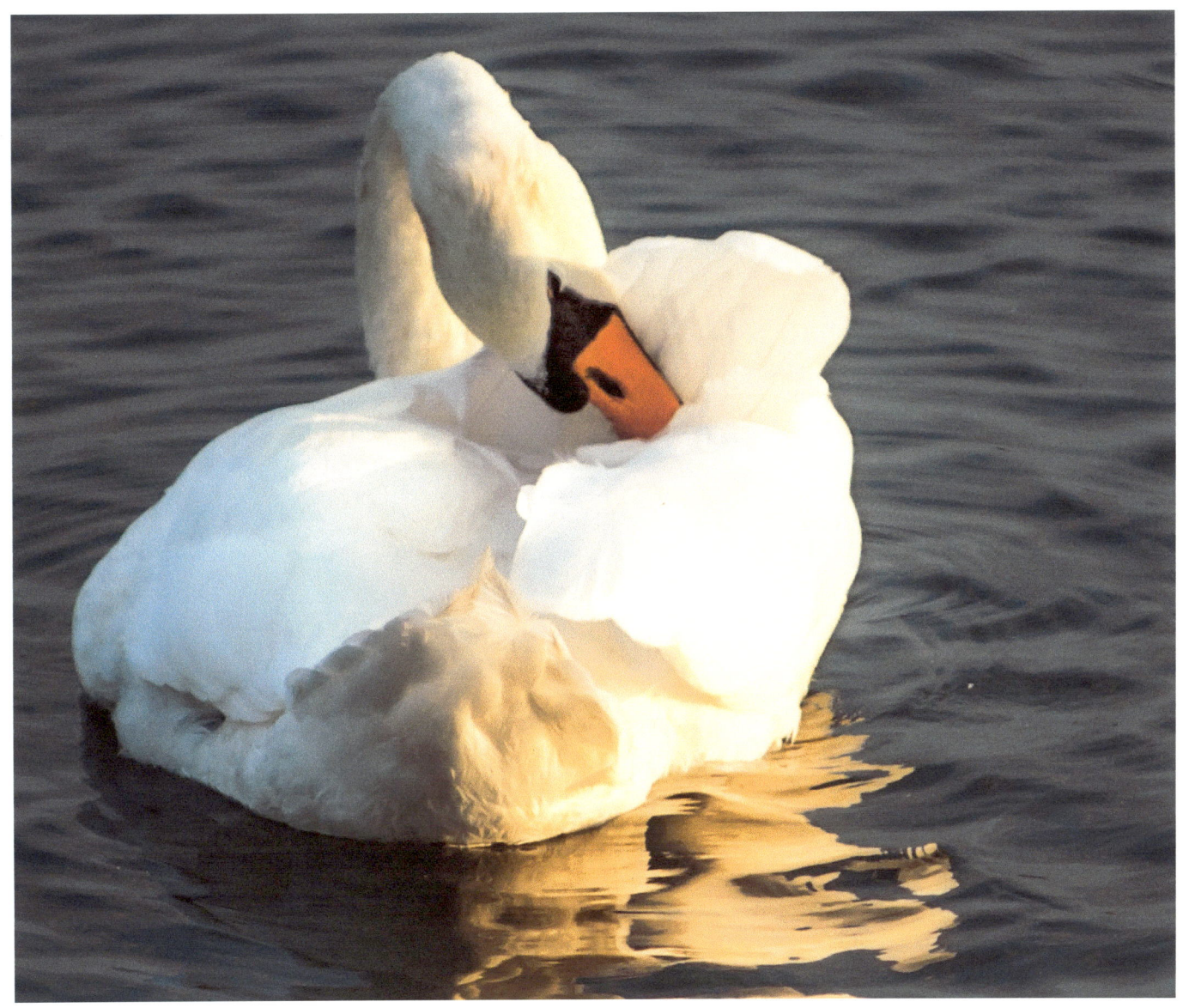

A Swan Dance - Mute Swan - Exposing Long, Mobile Neck

"The Donkey Walks"

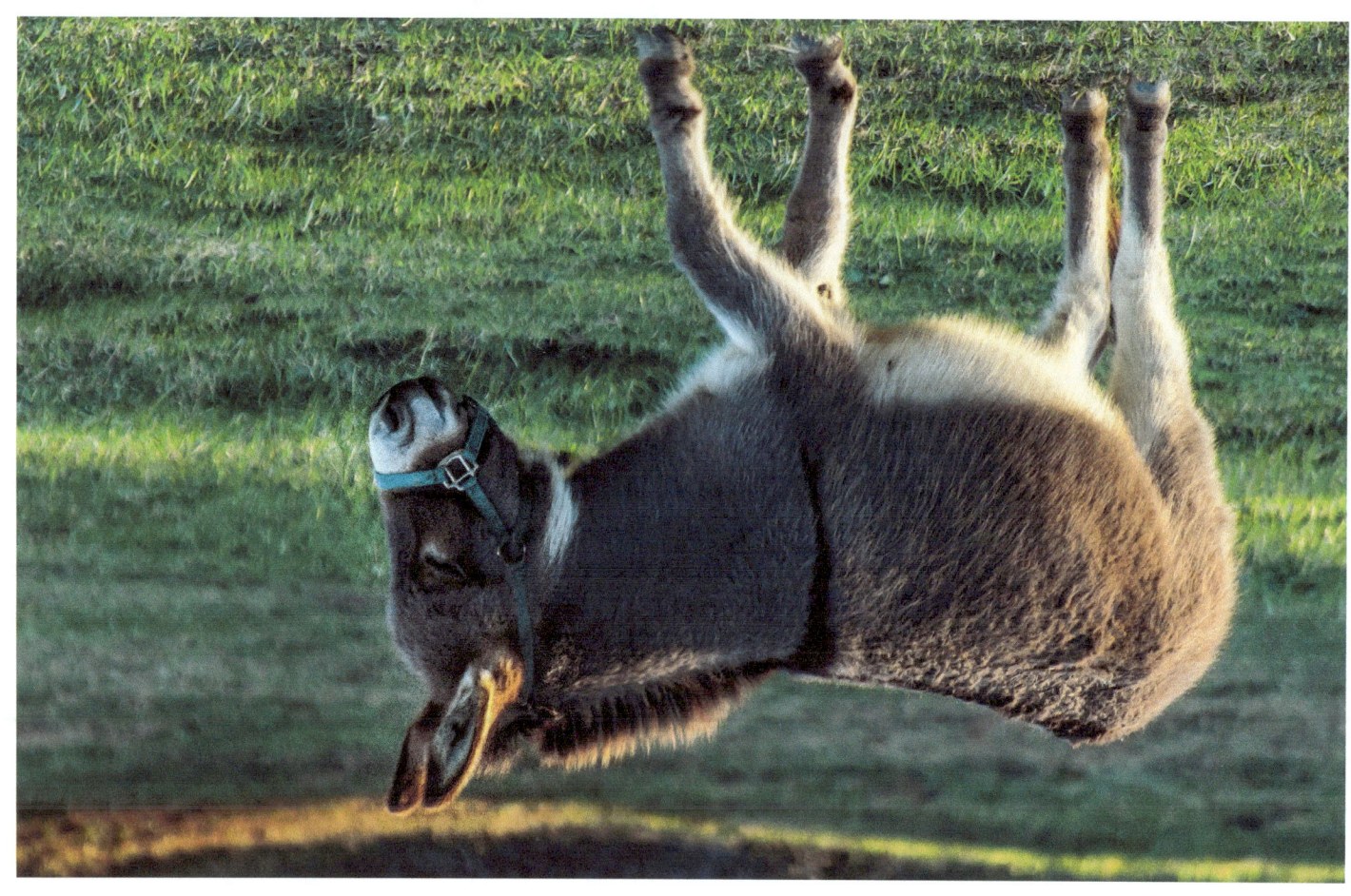

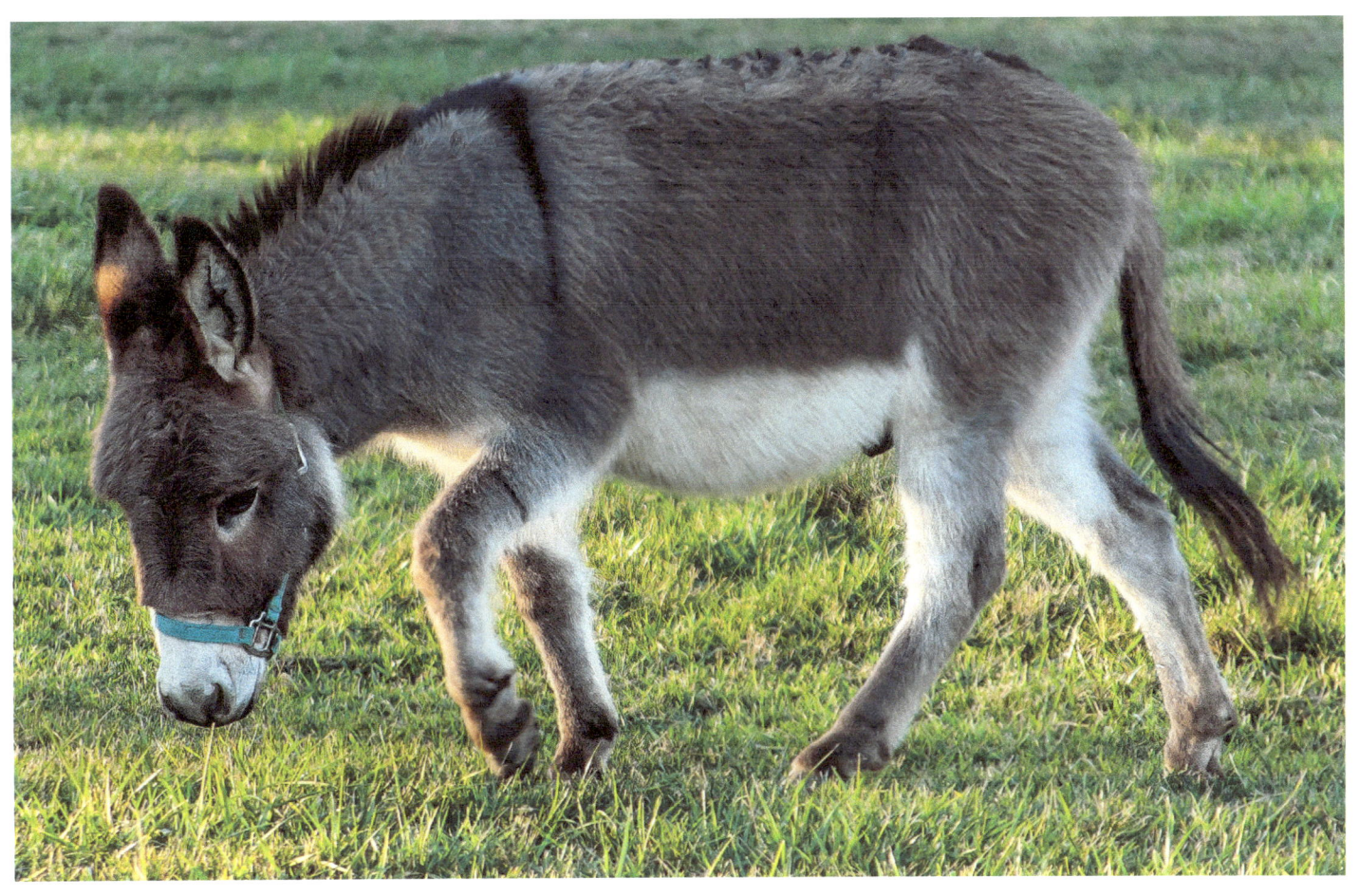

"The Donkey Runs"

Equestrian at Salamander Resort & Spa, Middleburg, VA

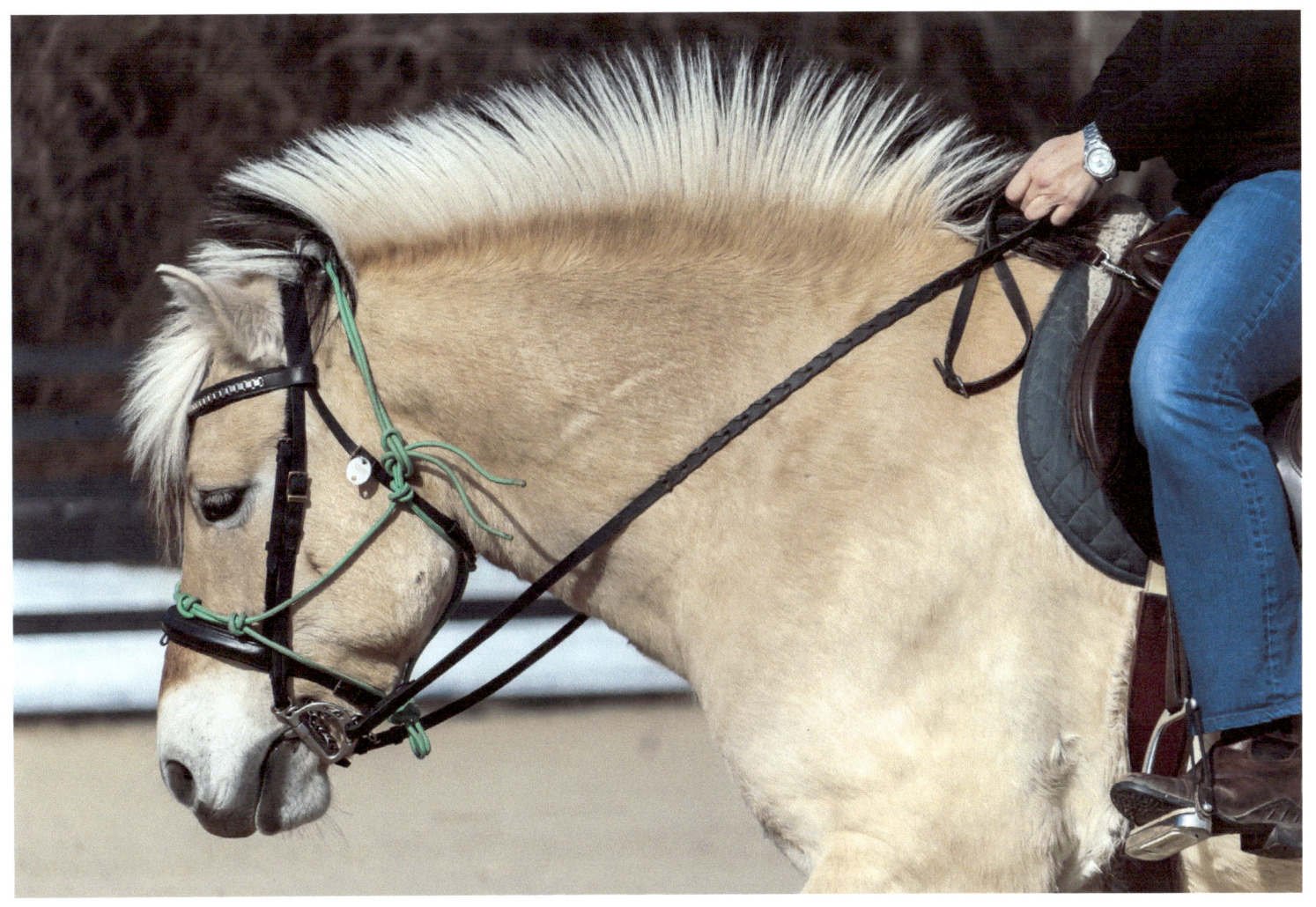

A Stunning Palomino Horse

An Observing Peacock

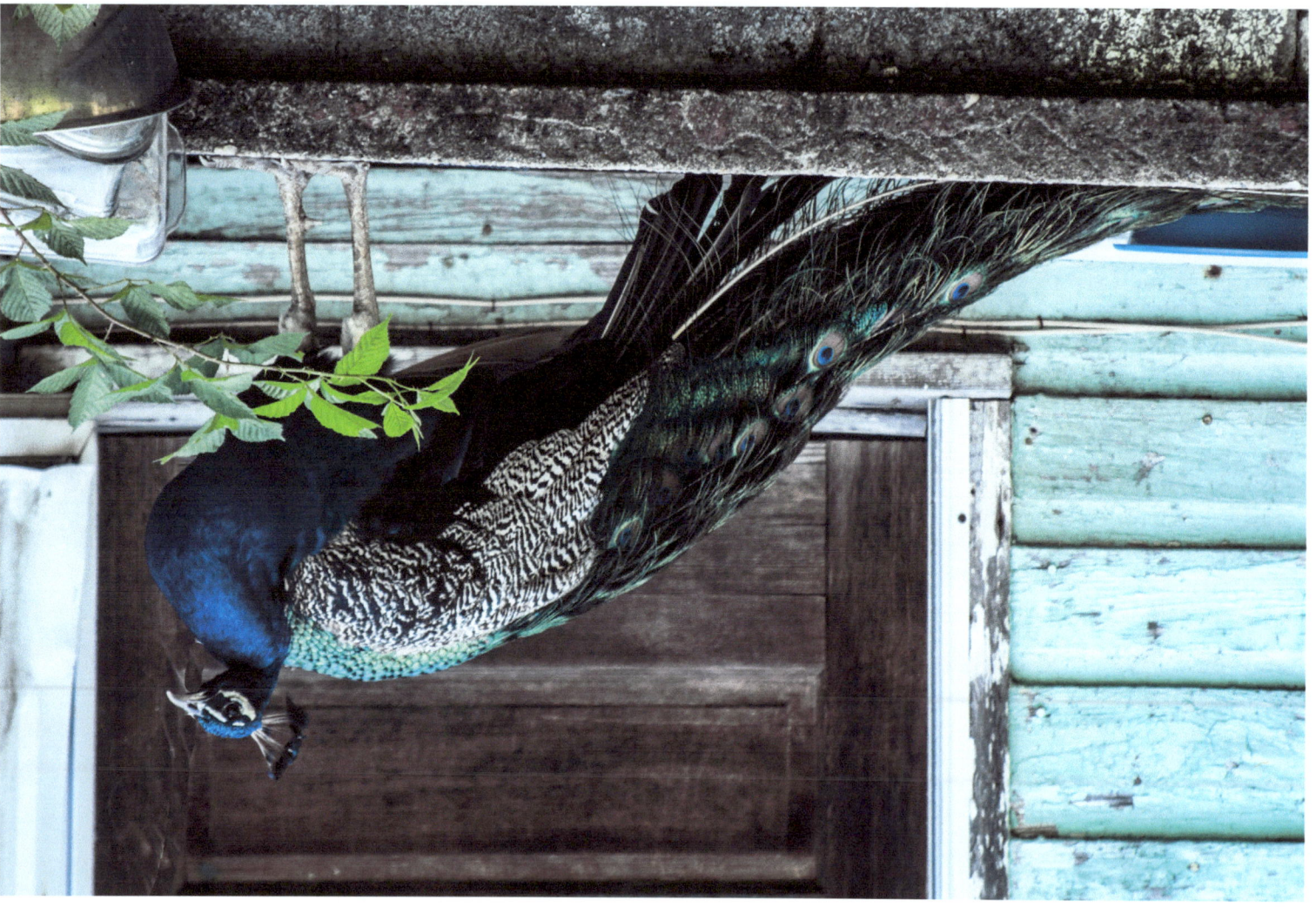

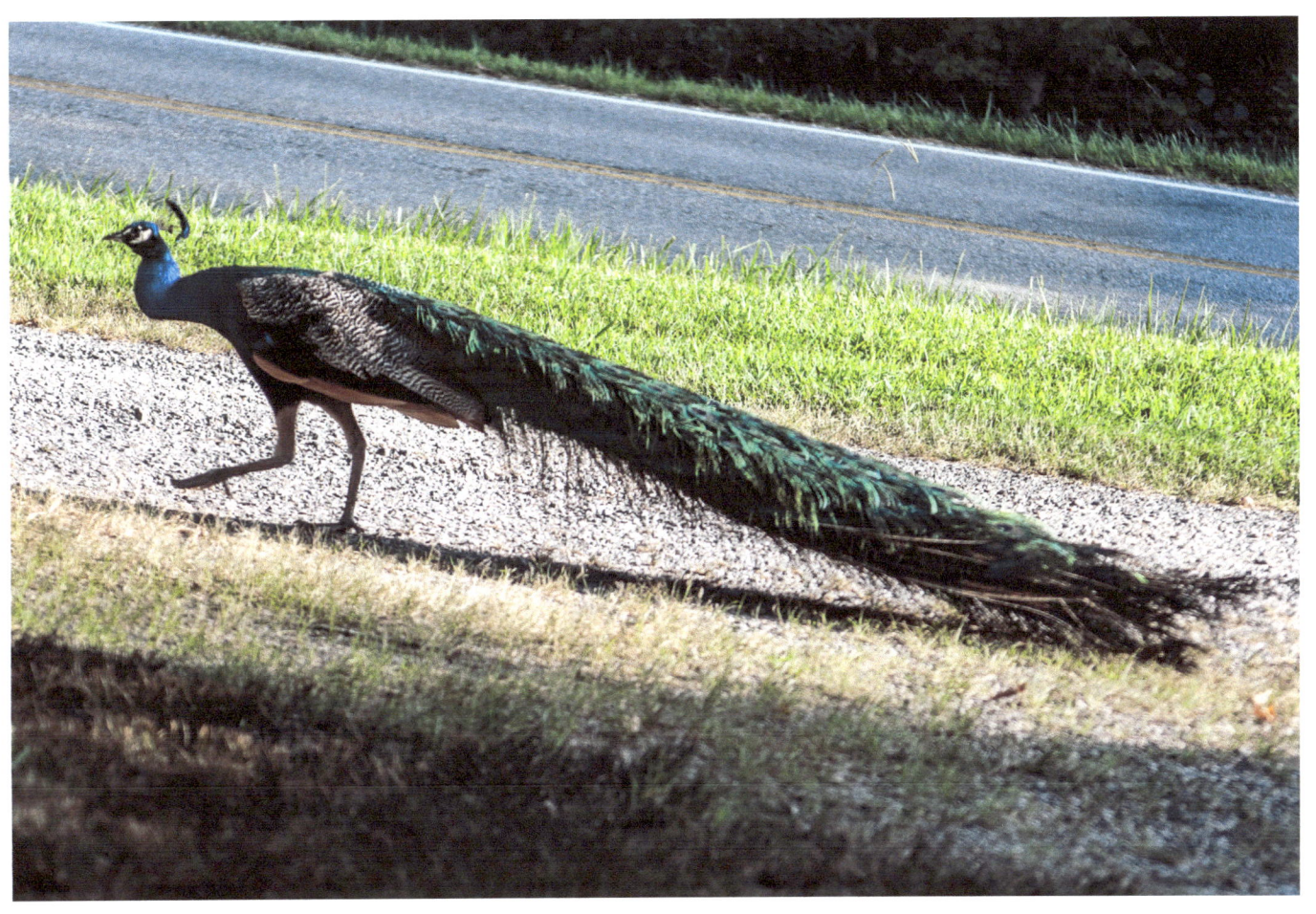

A Wandering Peacock

Hen "Struts Her Stuff"

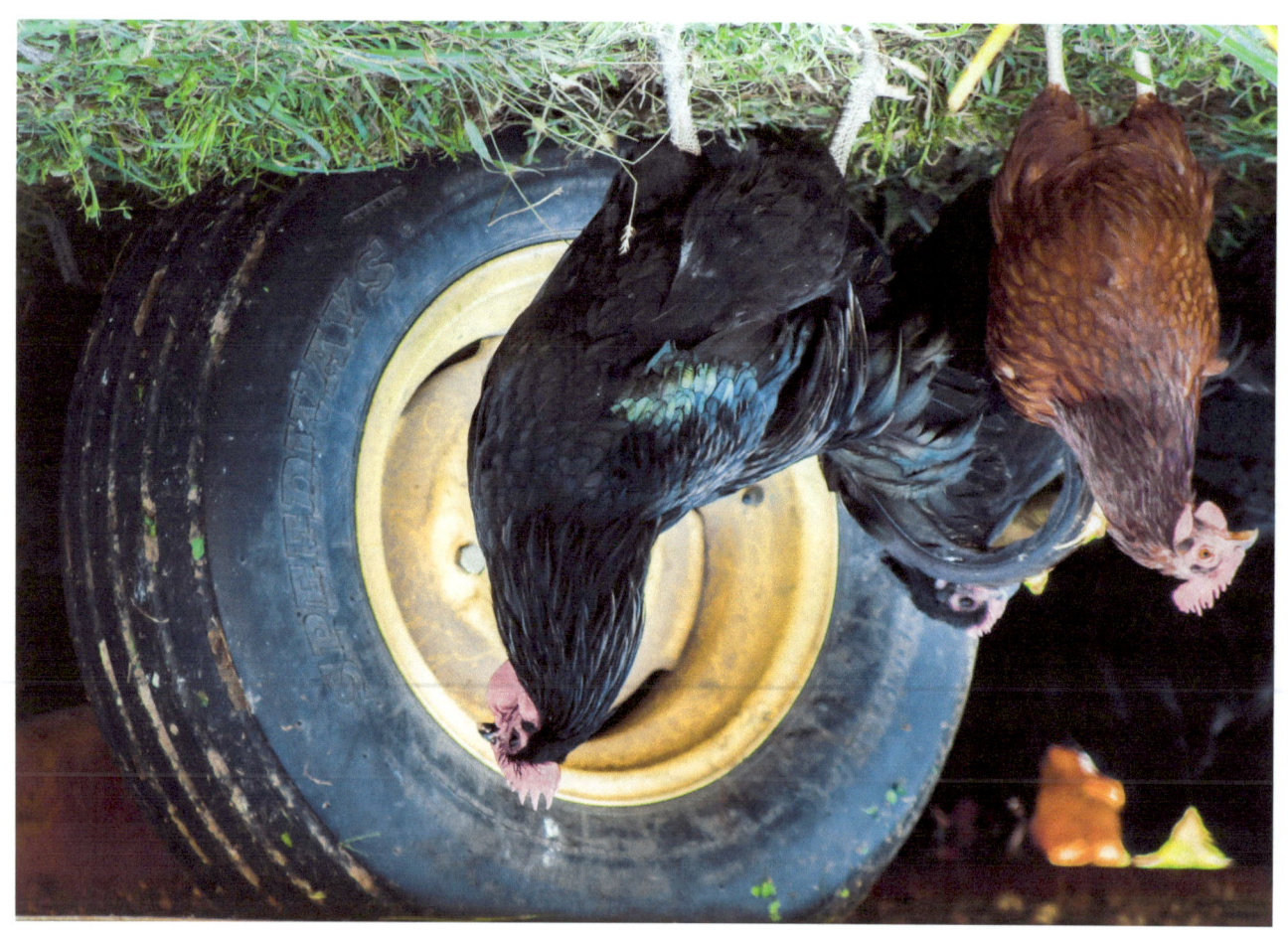

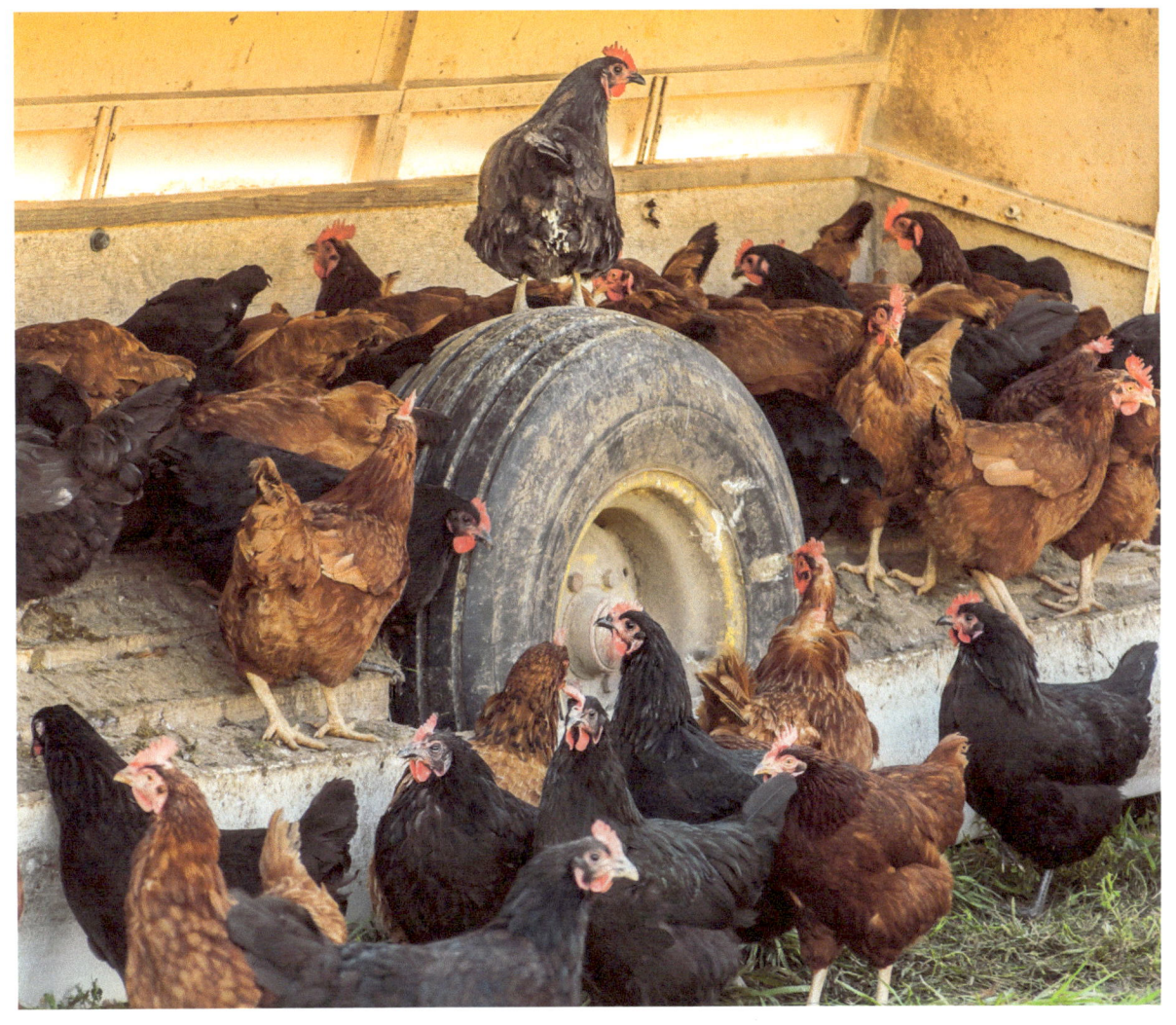

Hen "Rules the Roost"

A Rider's Dream

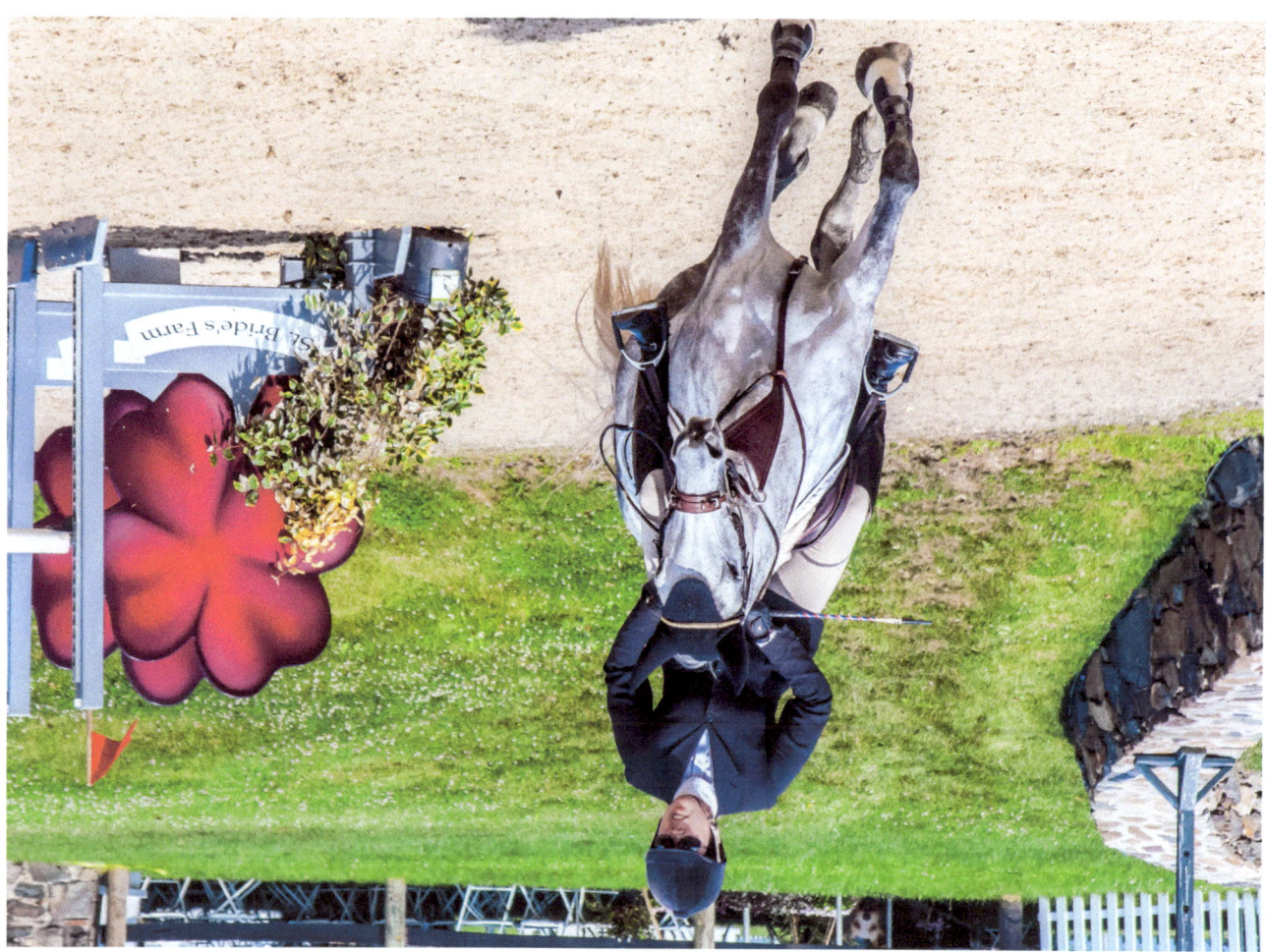

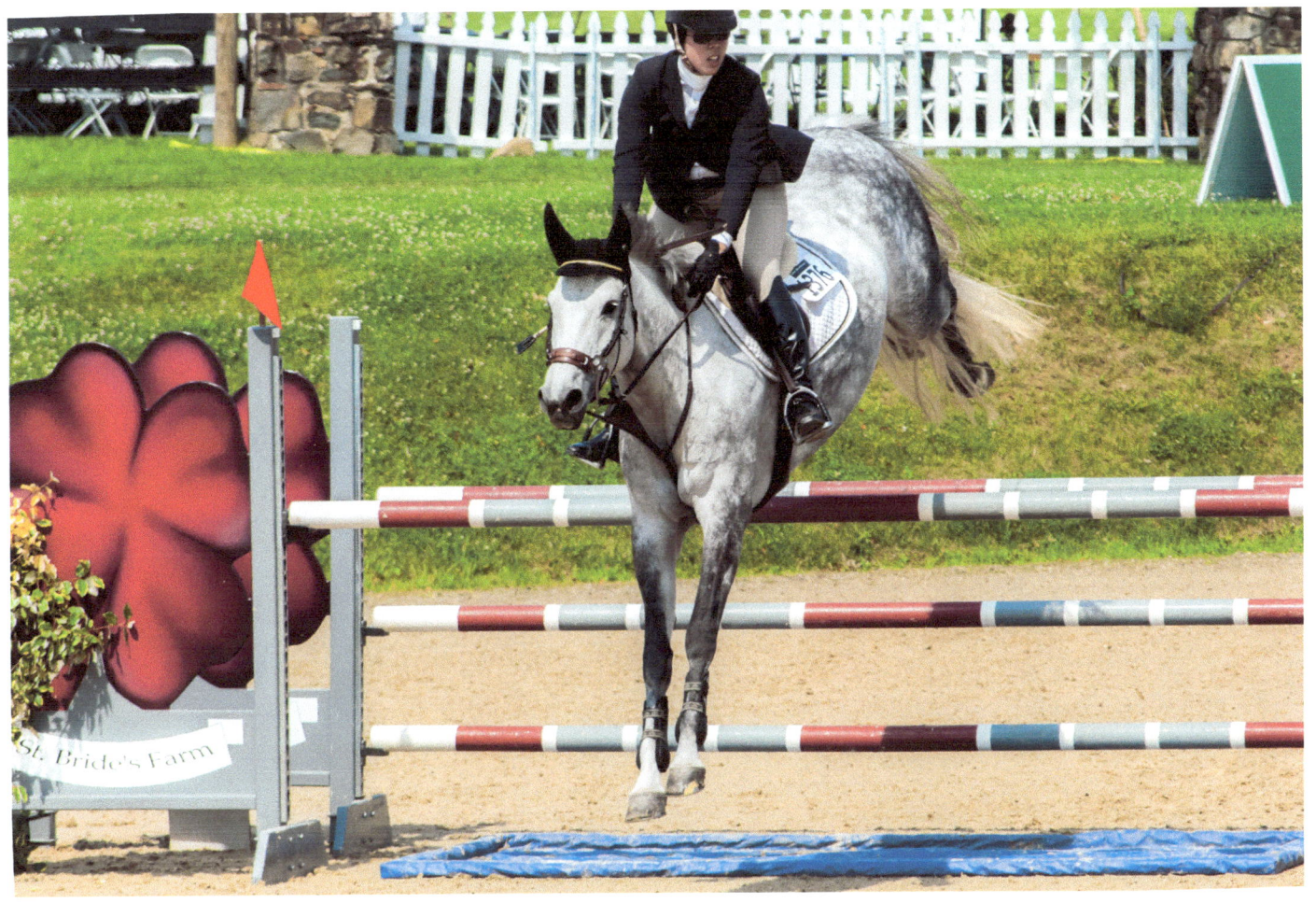

Artistic Beauty

Welcoming Monument - Rockingham County Turkey Capital

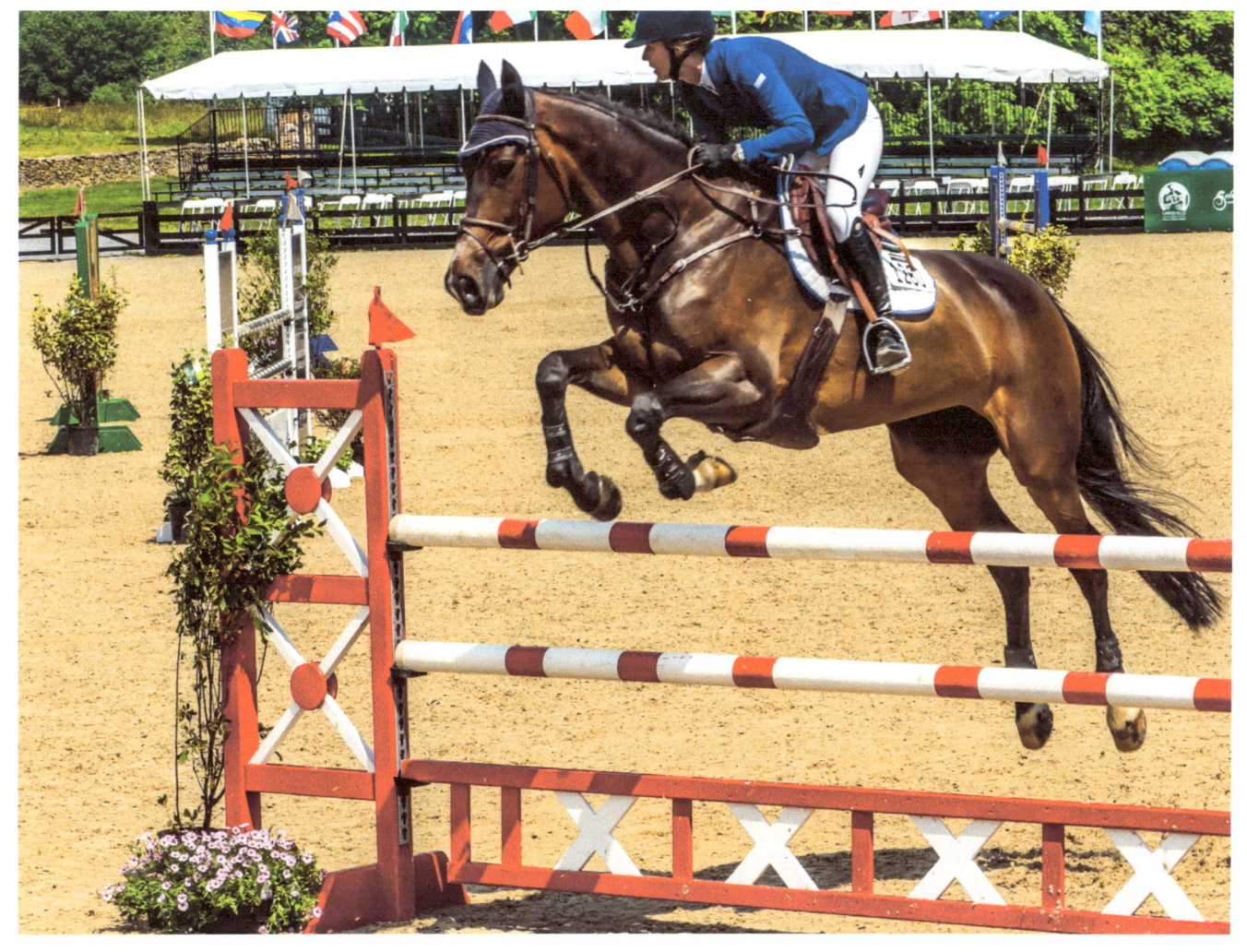

A Performing Horse at the Upperville Colt and Horse Show

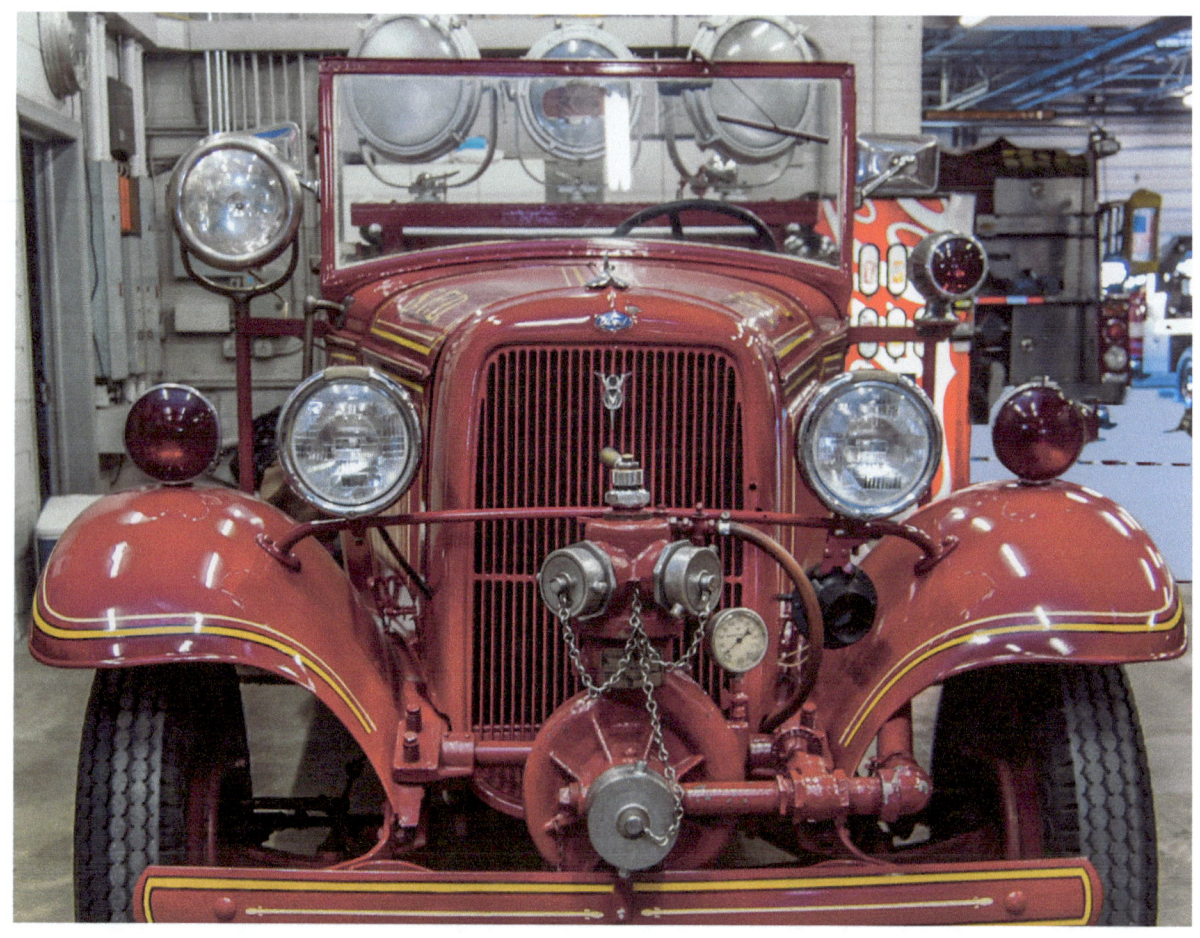

1934 Ford Oren Firetruck in Strasburg, Virginia (Frontal View)

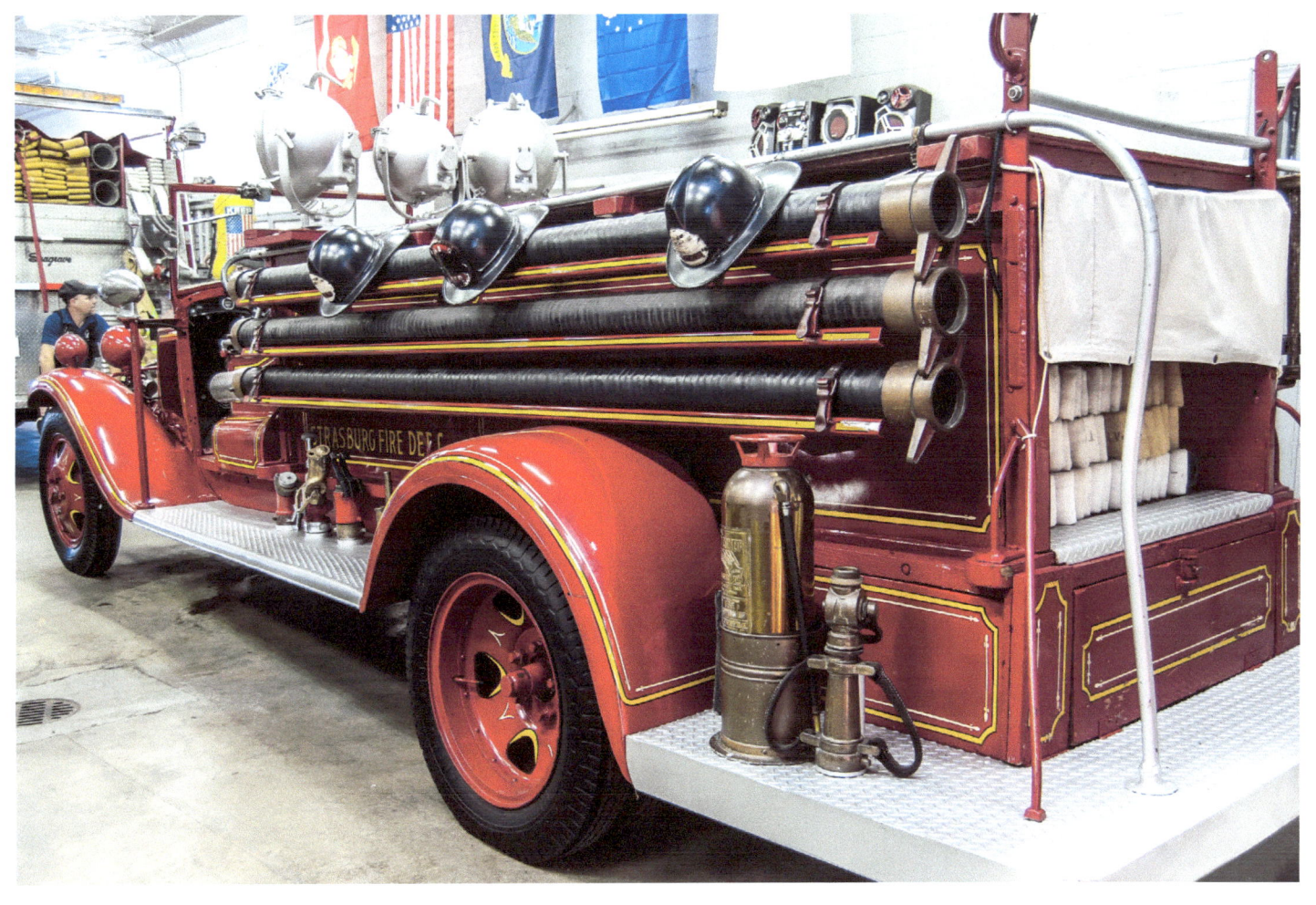

1934 Ford Oren Firetruck in Strasburg, Virginia (Side View)

A Close Up View of a Buggy in Dayton, Virginia

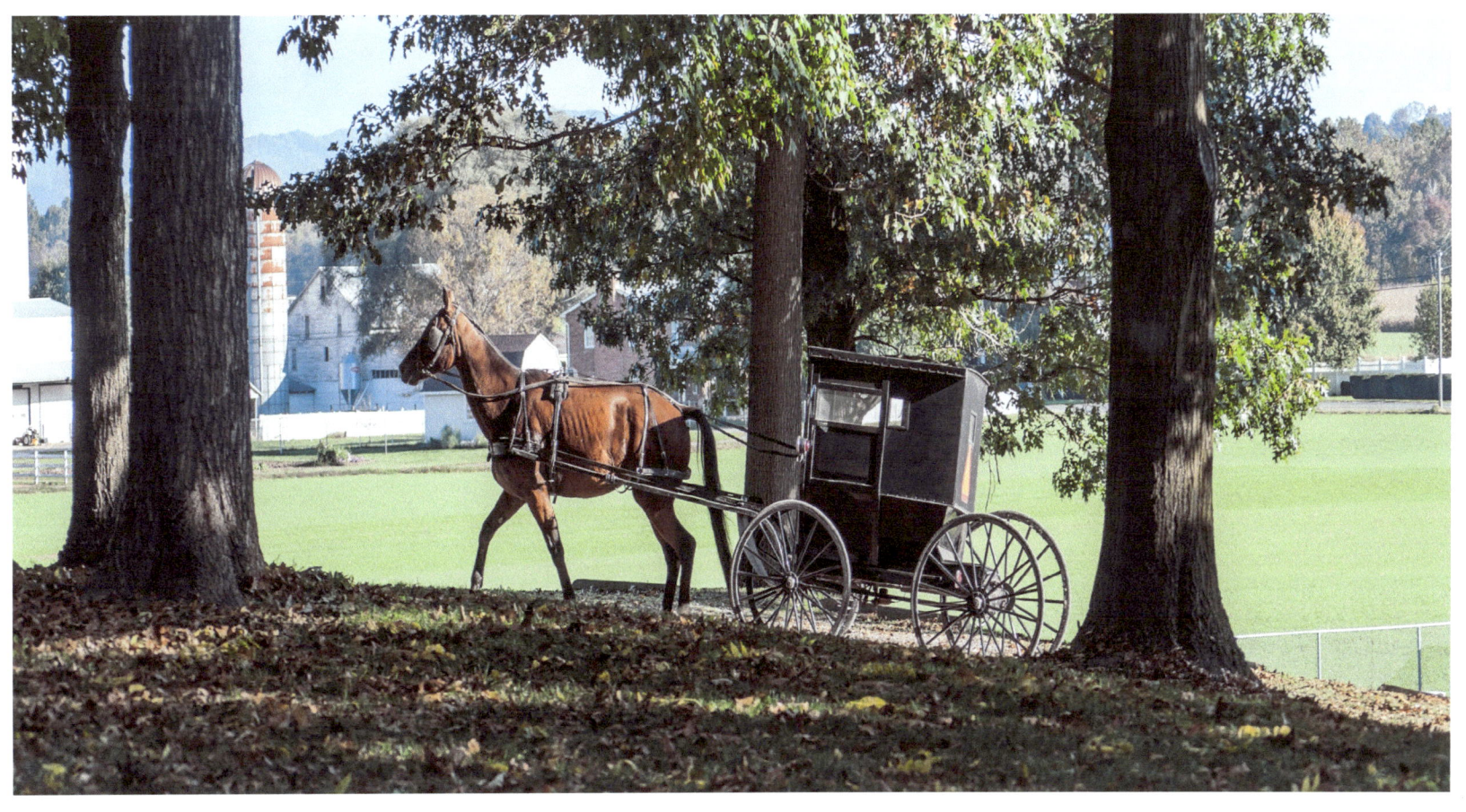

A Picturesque View in Dayton, Virginia

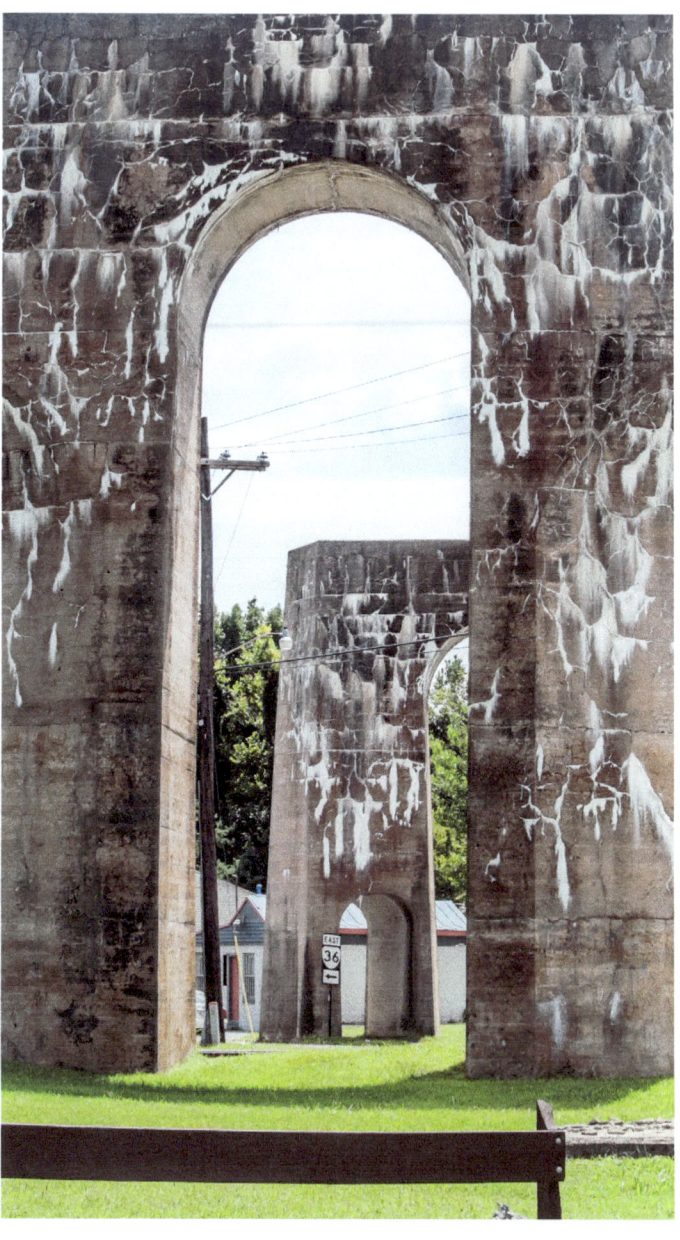

Ruins from Concrete Buttresses, Original Railway Arches, Campbell's Bridge in Ettrick, Virginia

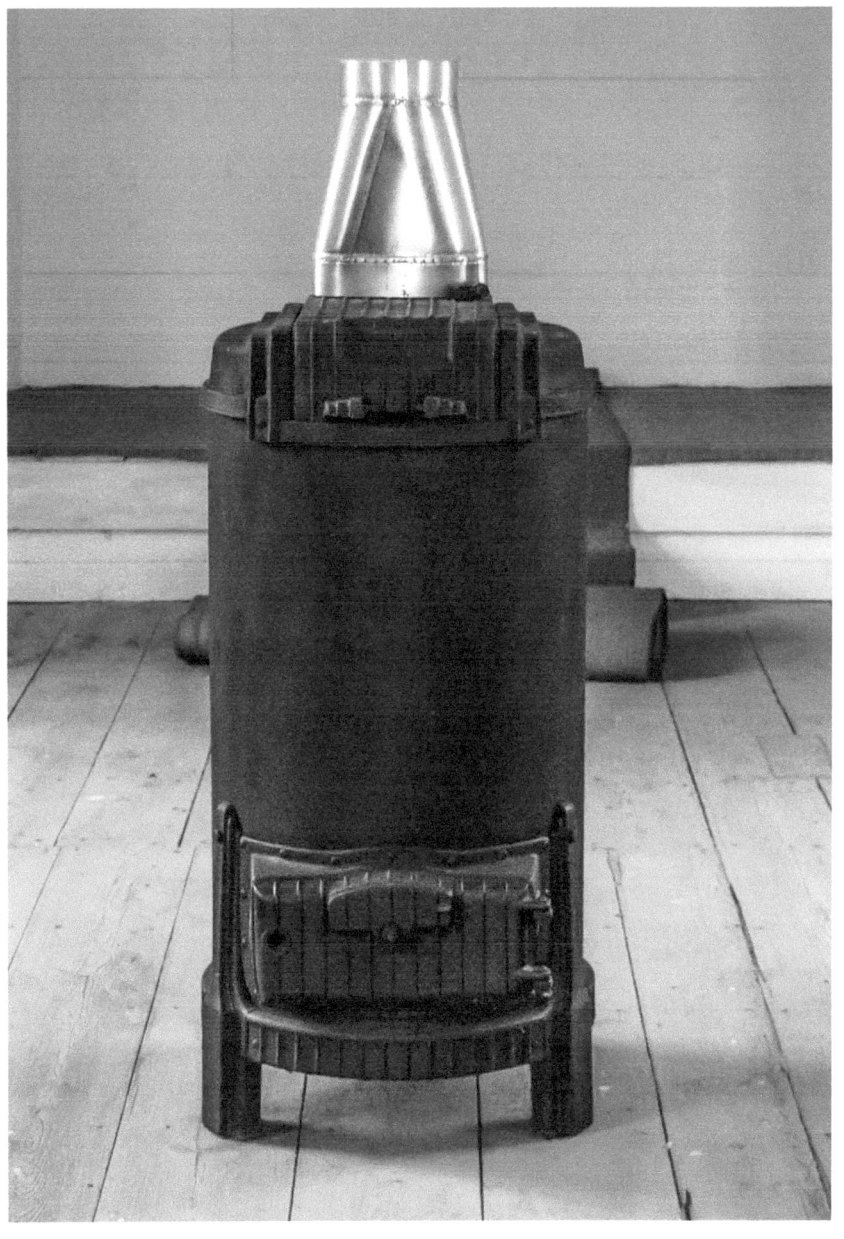
Antique Space Heater (1870) - Long Chapel at Zenda in Harrisonburg, Virginia

Vintage Car Sofa Seat - Yellow

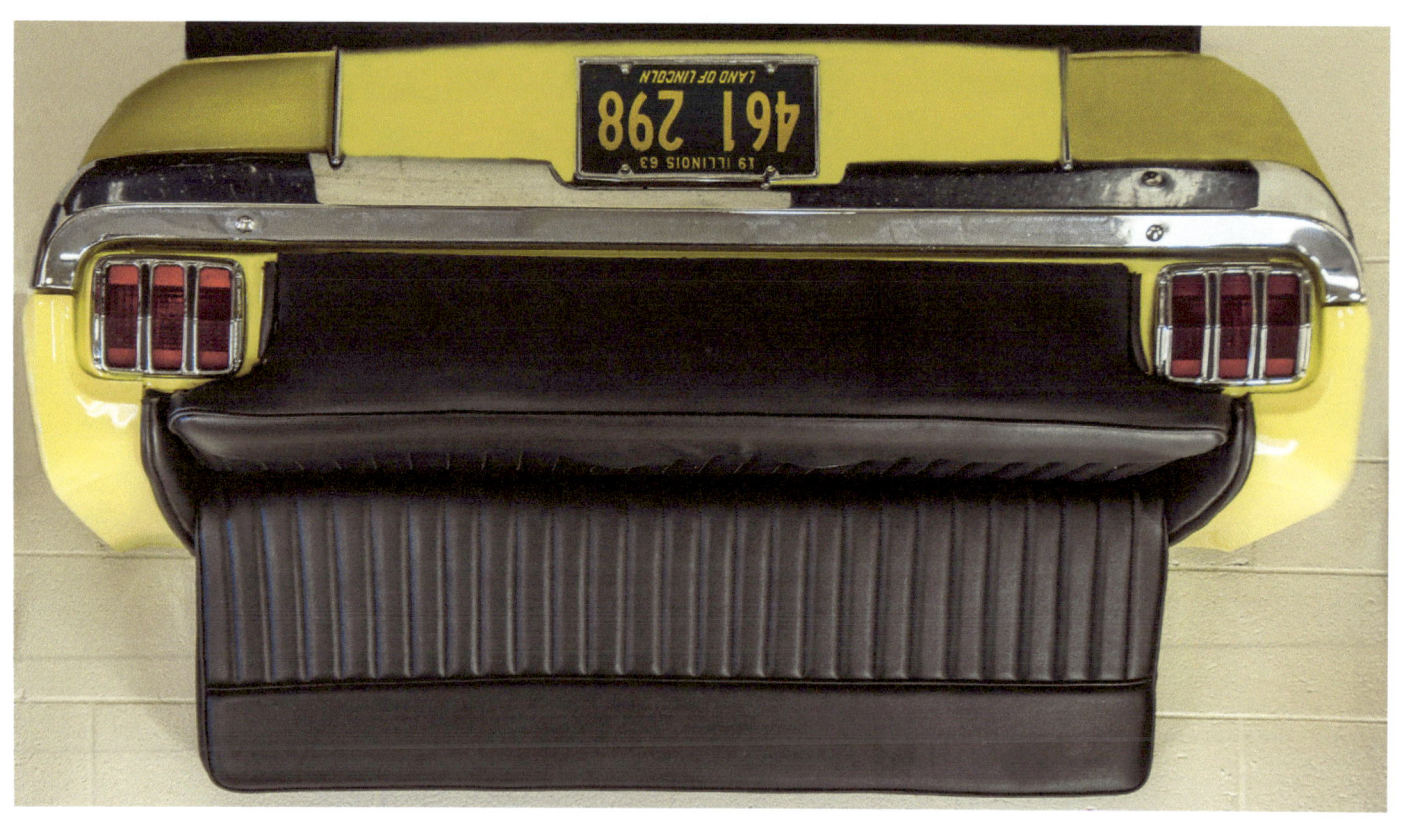

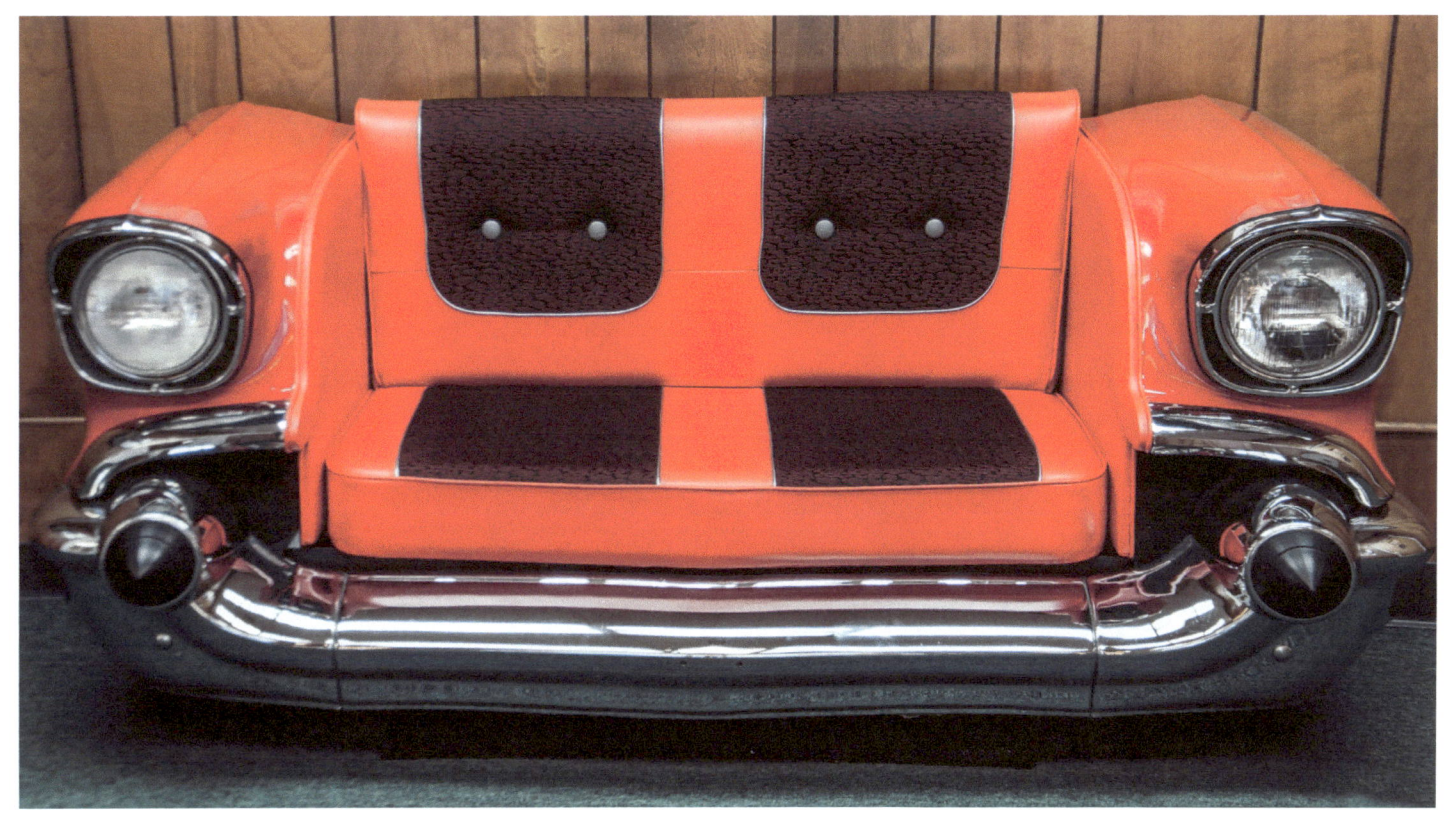

Vintage Car Sofa Seat - Red

An Artful Vehicle

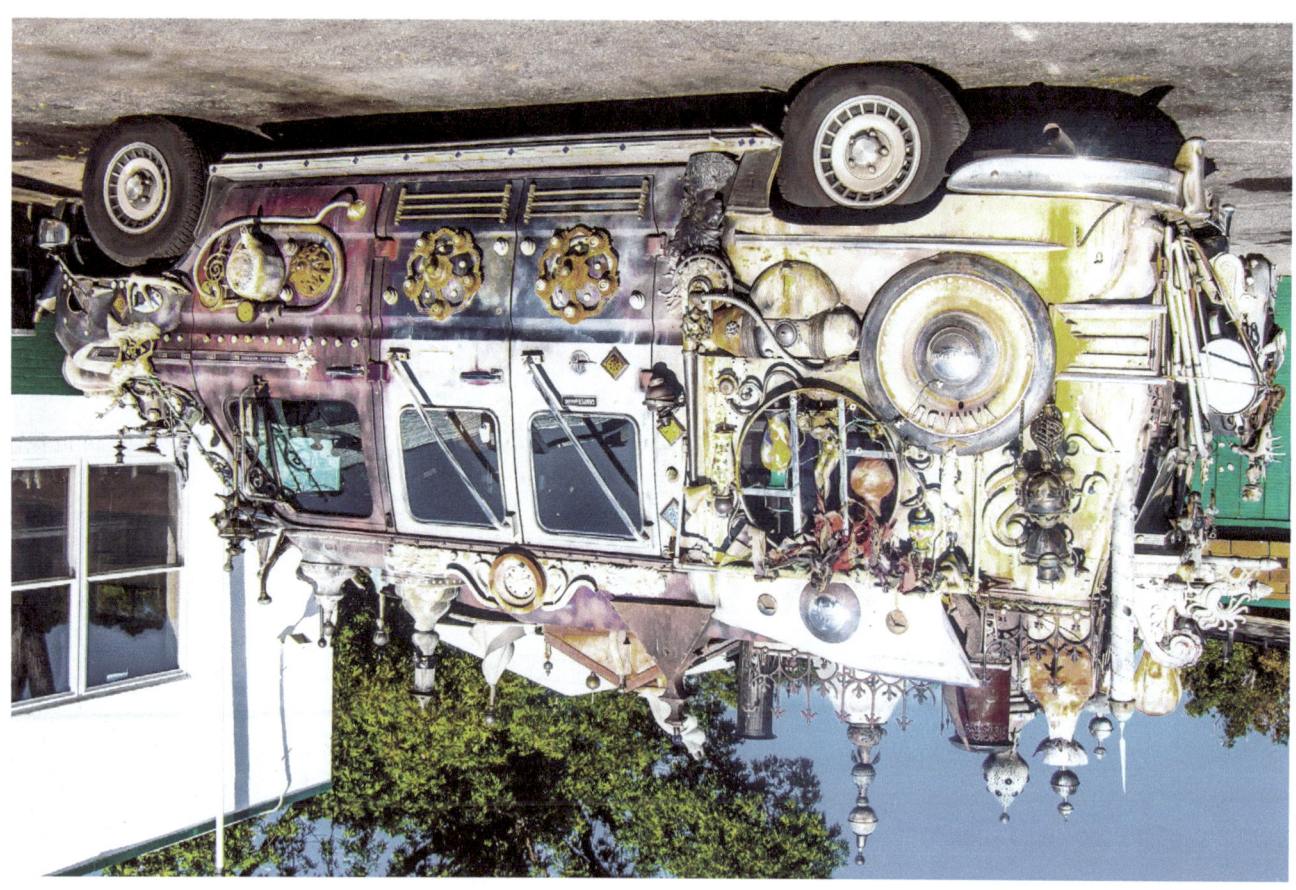

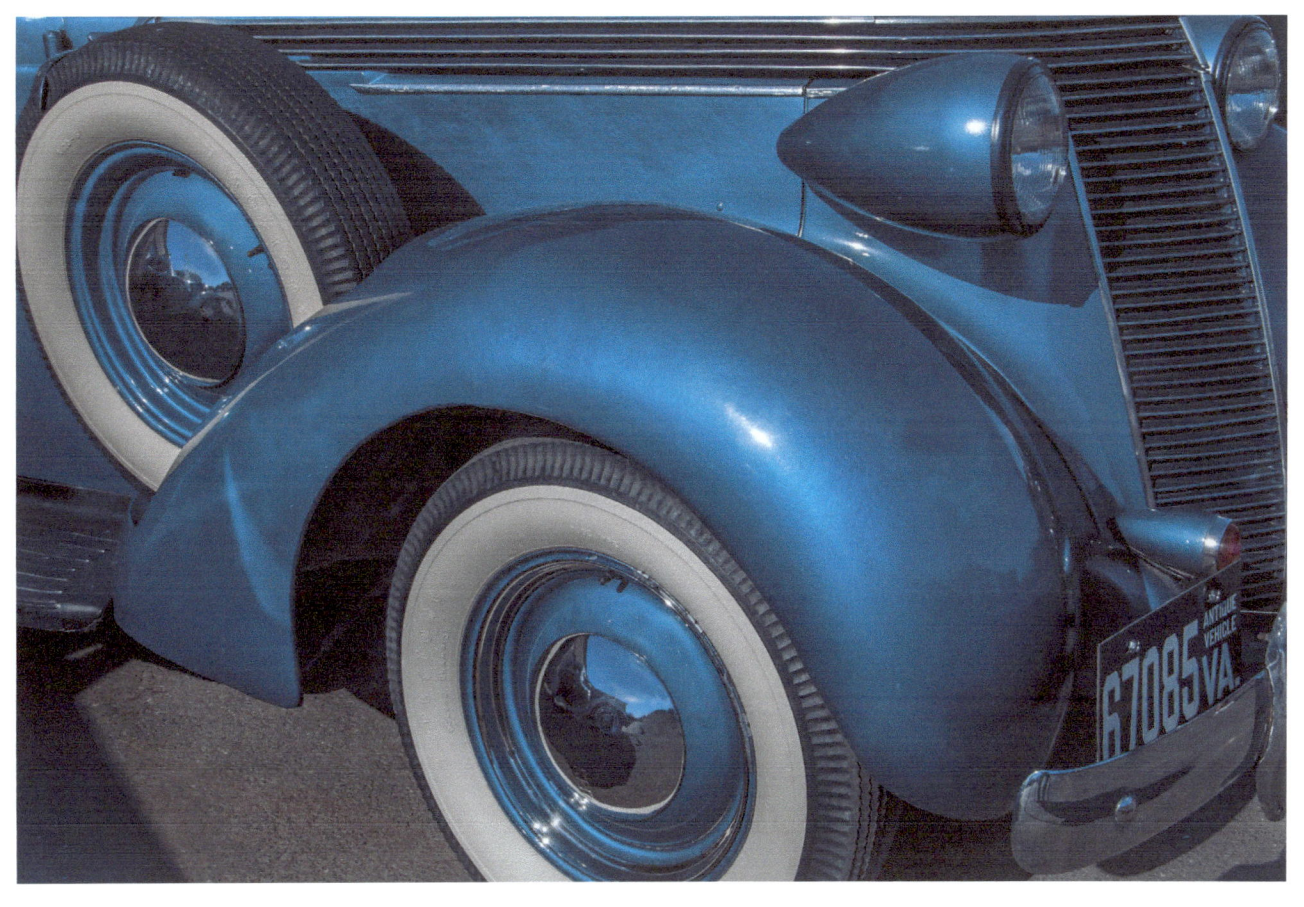

1937 Studebaker Coupe Express

Driving Wheel from Norfolk Southern D9-40CW9313

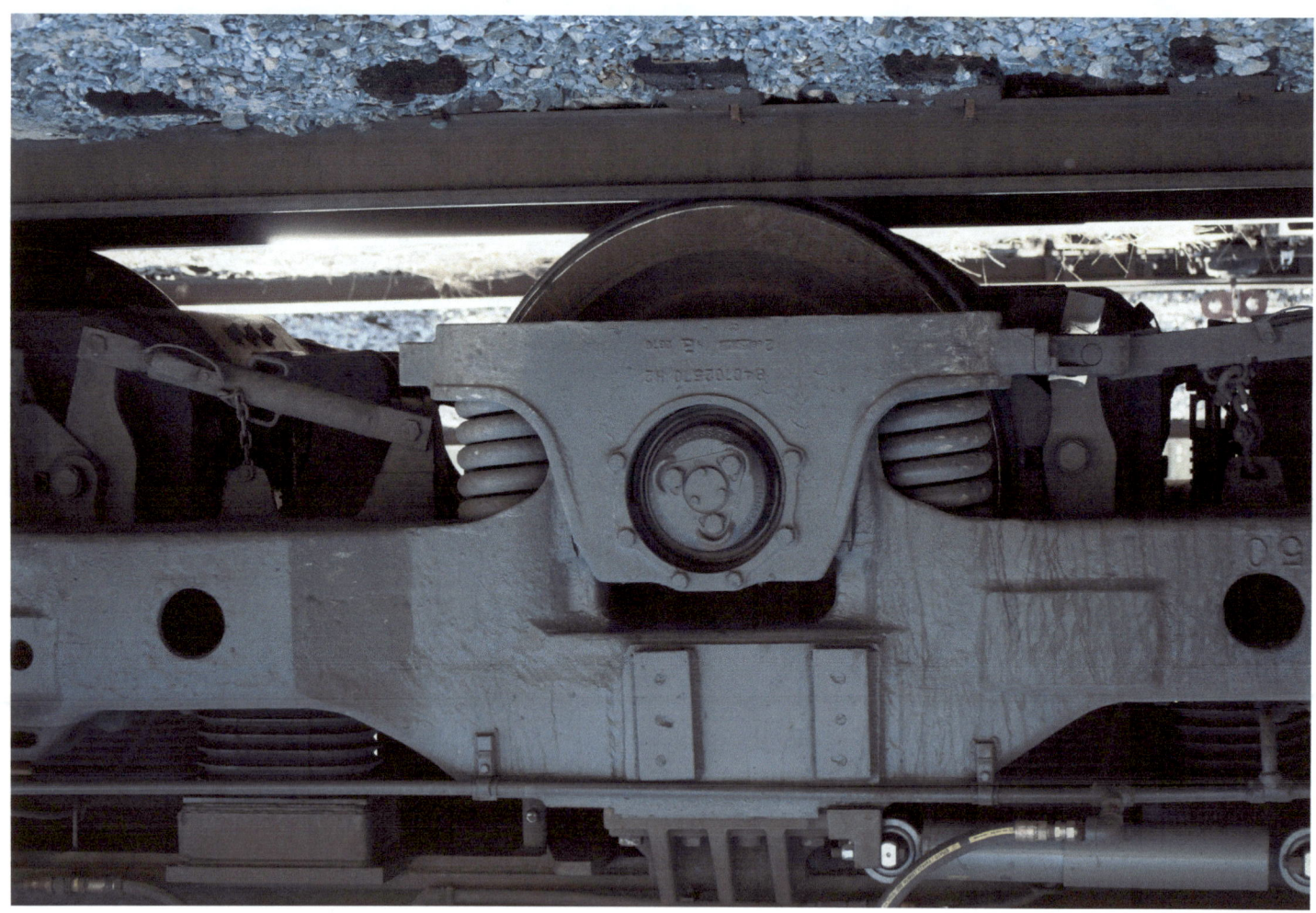

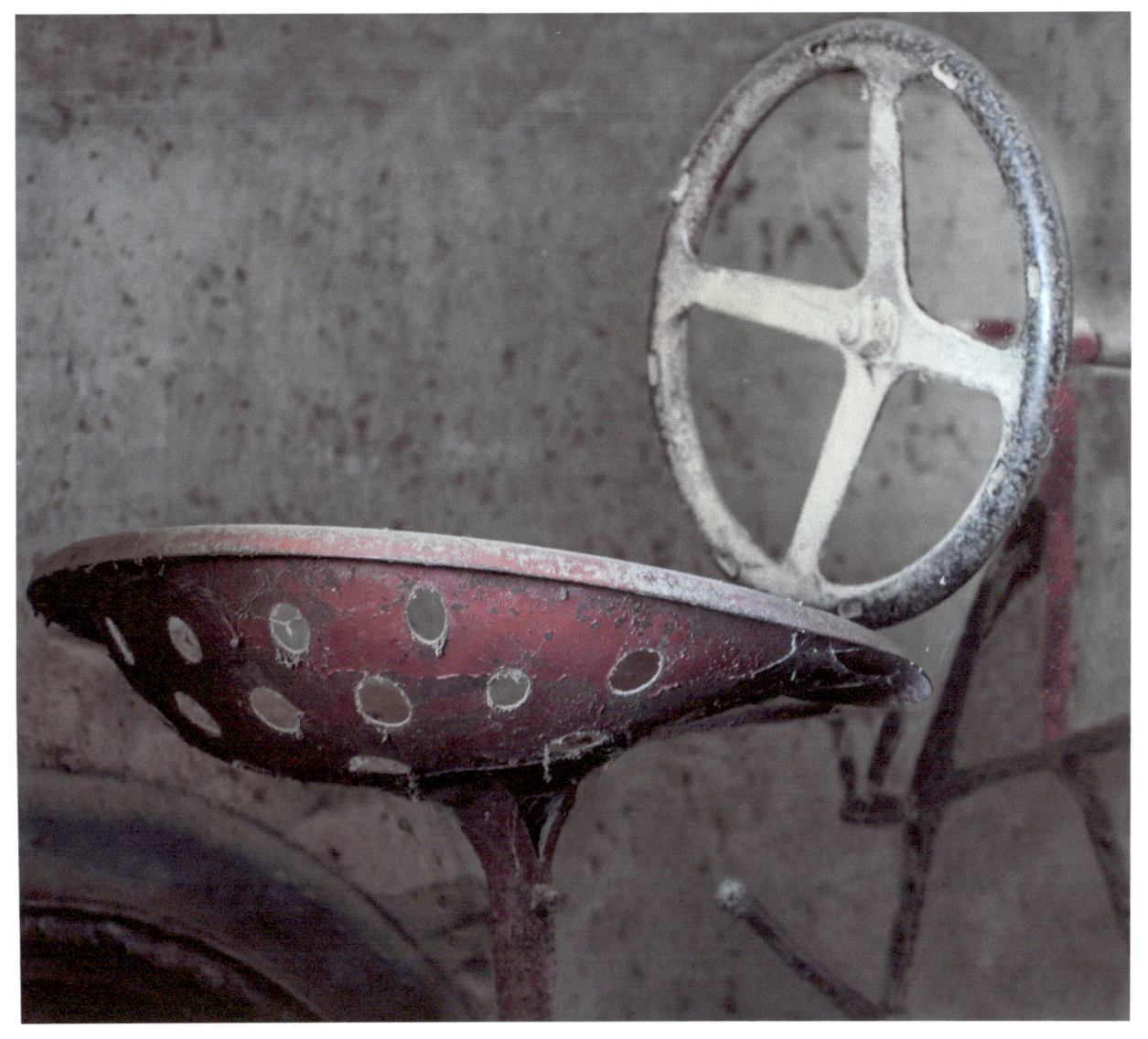

1941 Ford 9N Tractor Seat Pan & Steering Wheel in Dayton, Virginia

Historic House Near Dayton, Virginia

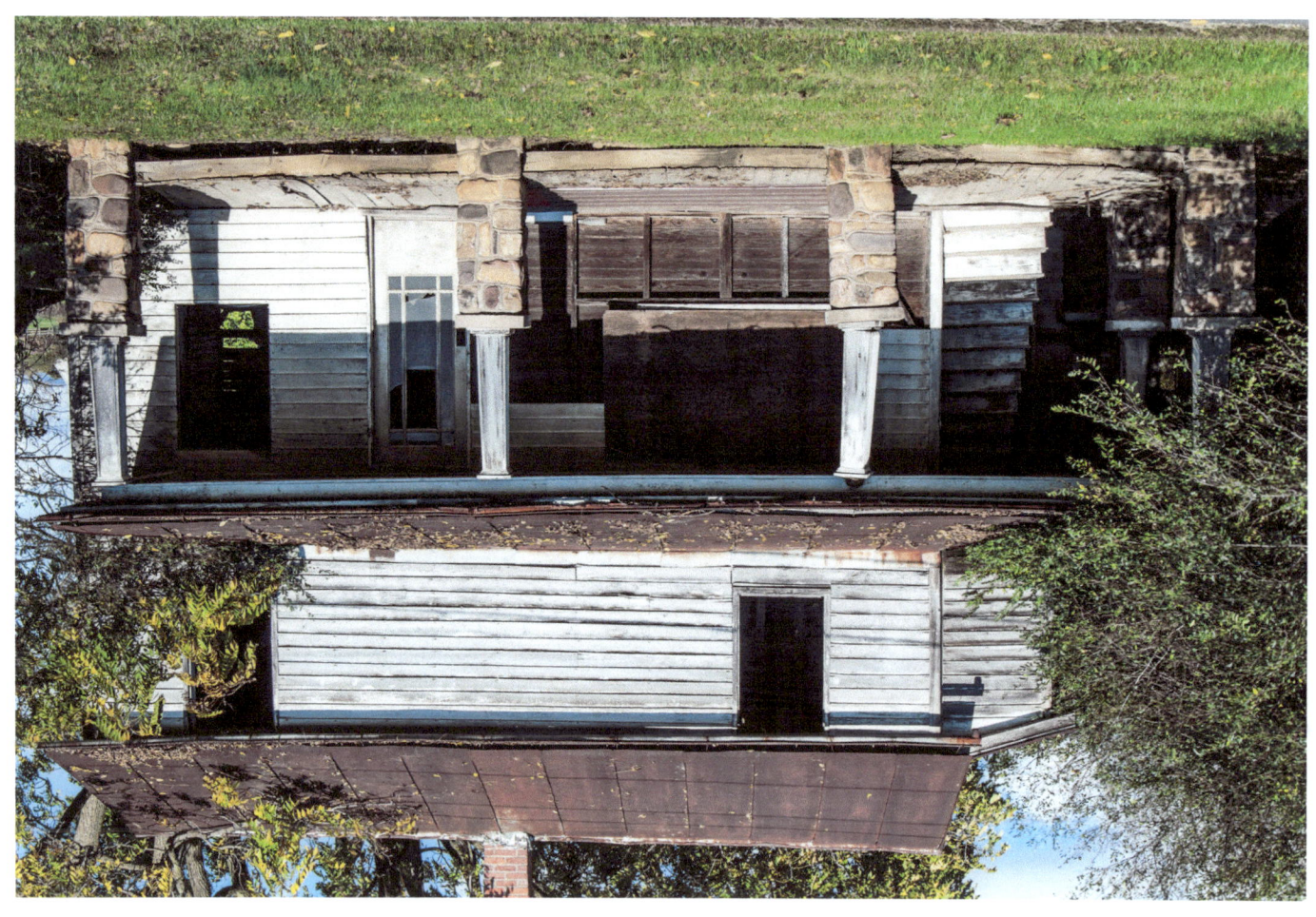

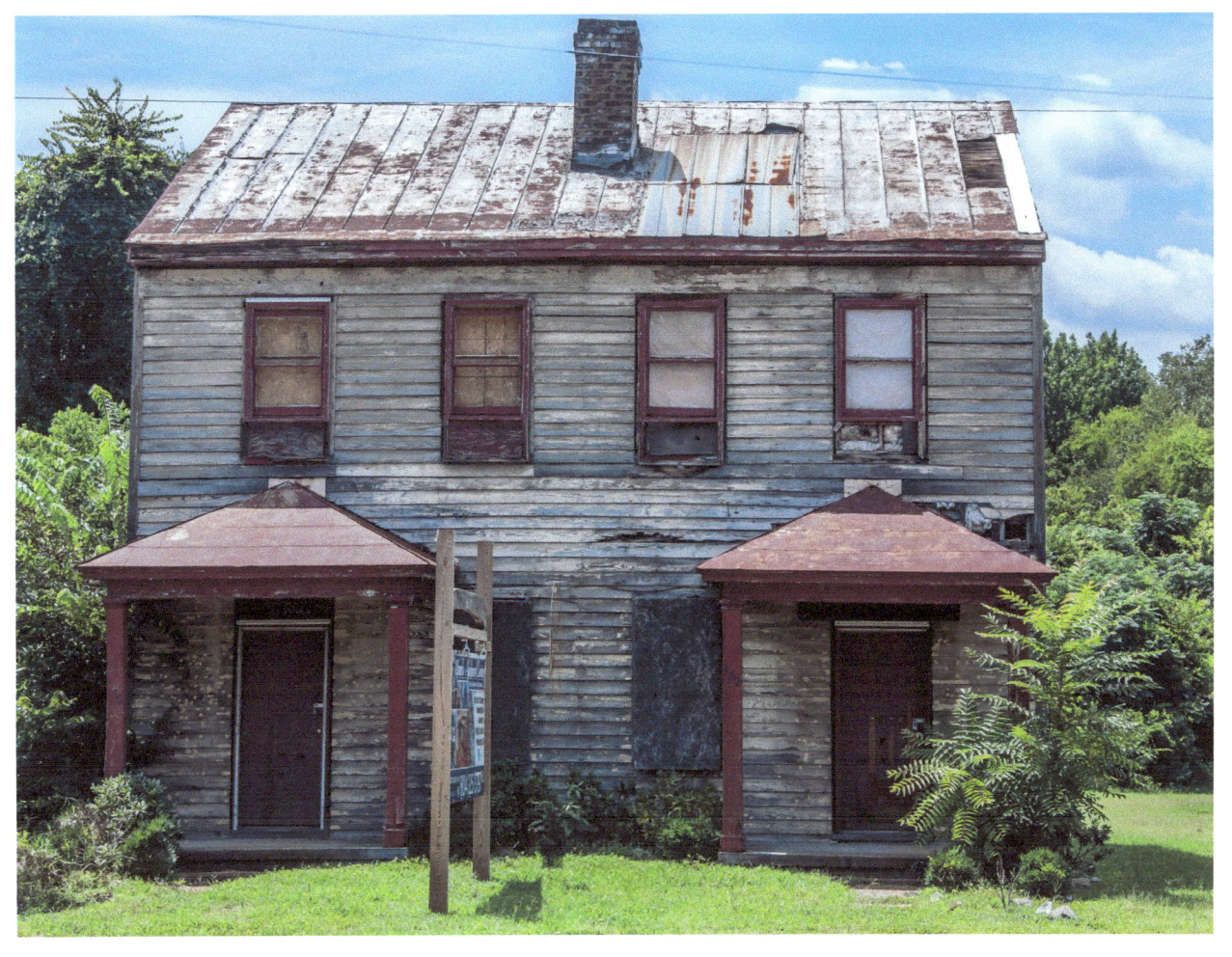

Historic House on Canal Street in Ettrick, Virginia

Closely Parked Buggies

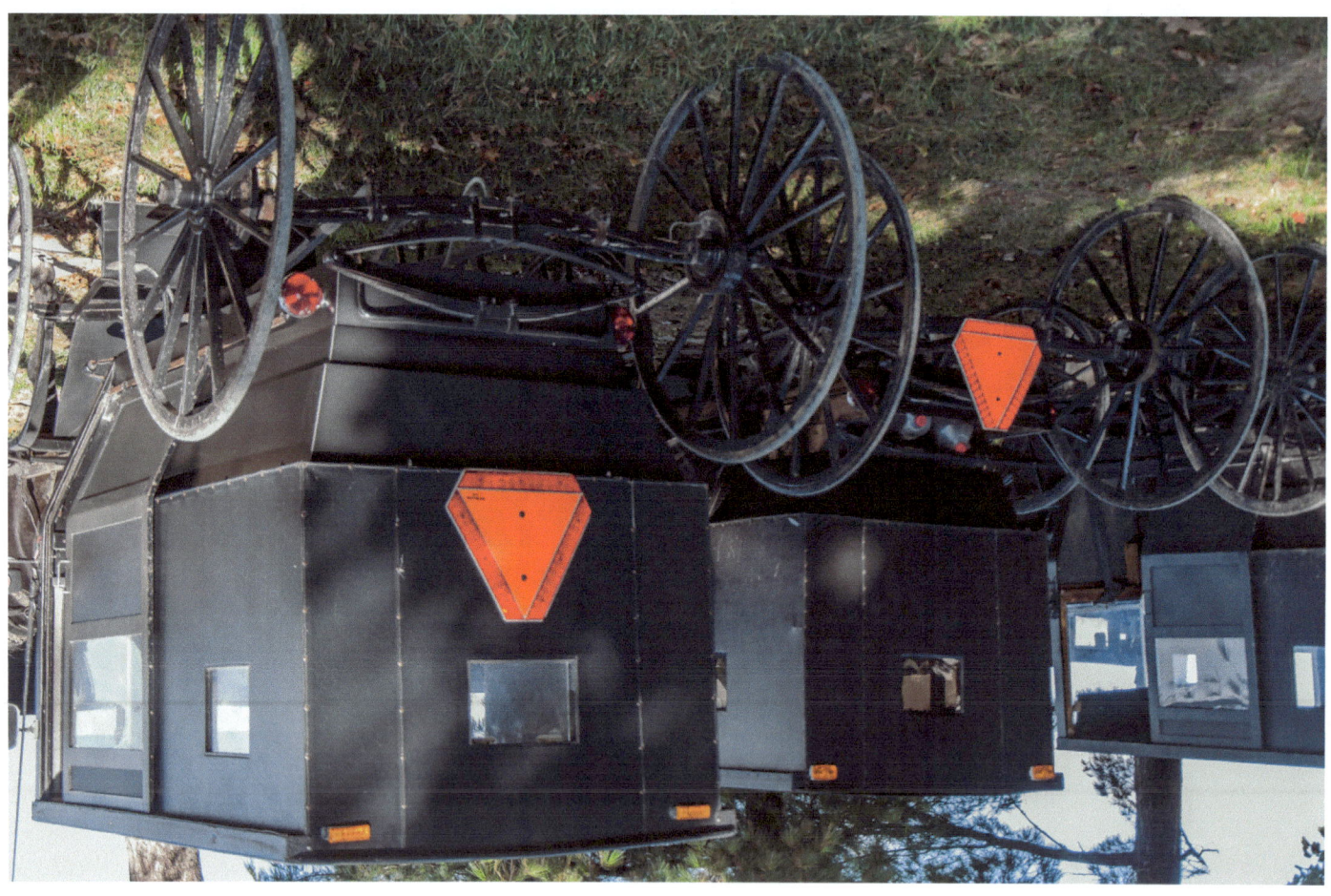

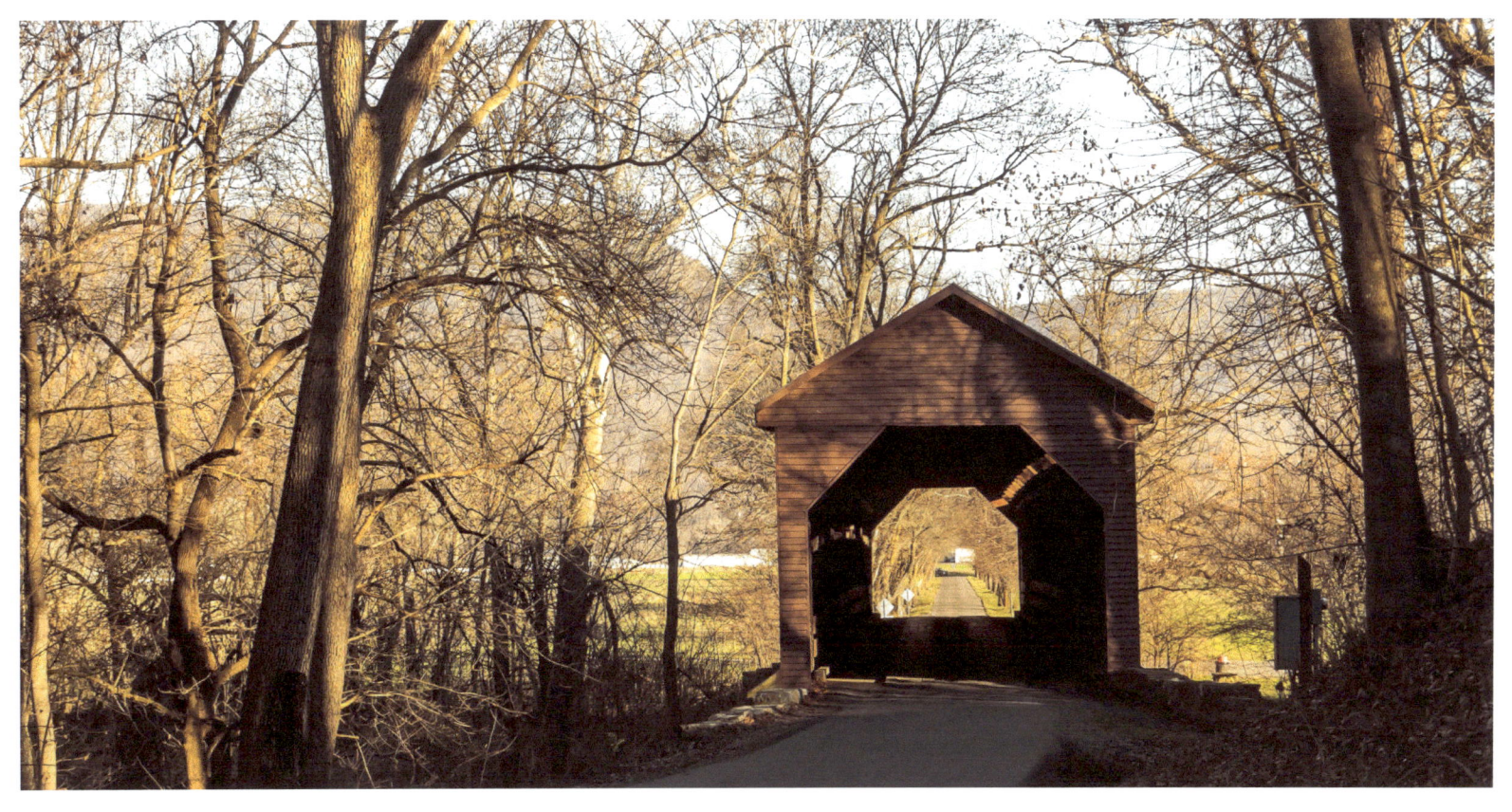

Meems Bottom Covered Bridge in Mt. Jackson, Virginia

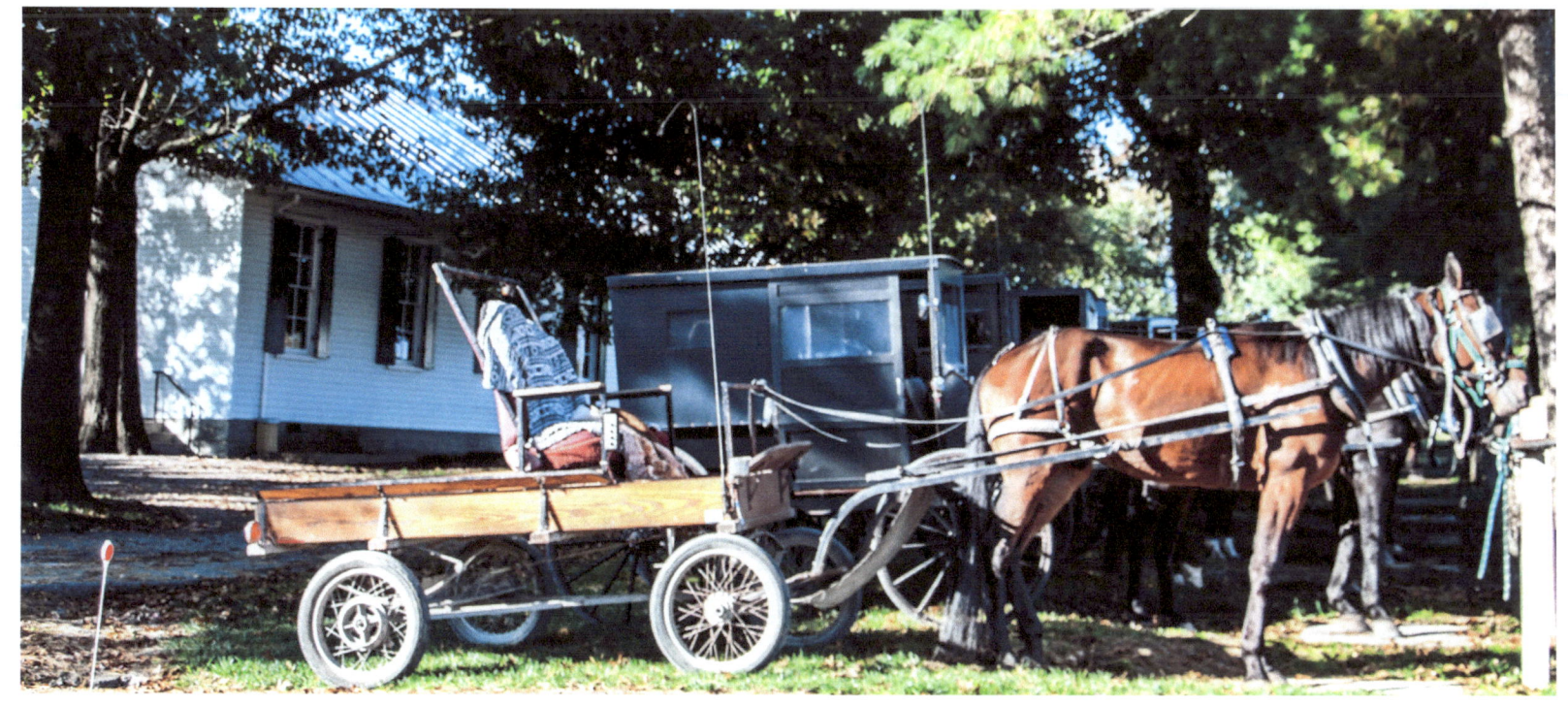

A Parked Horse-Driven Spring Wagon

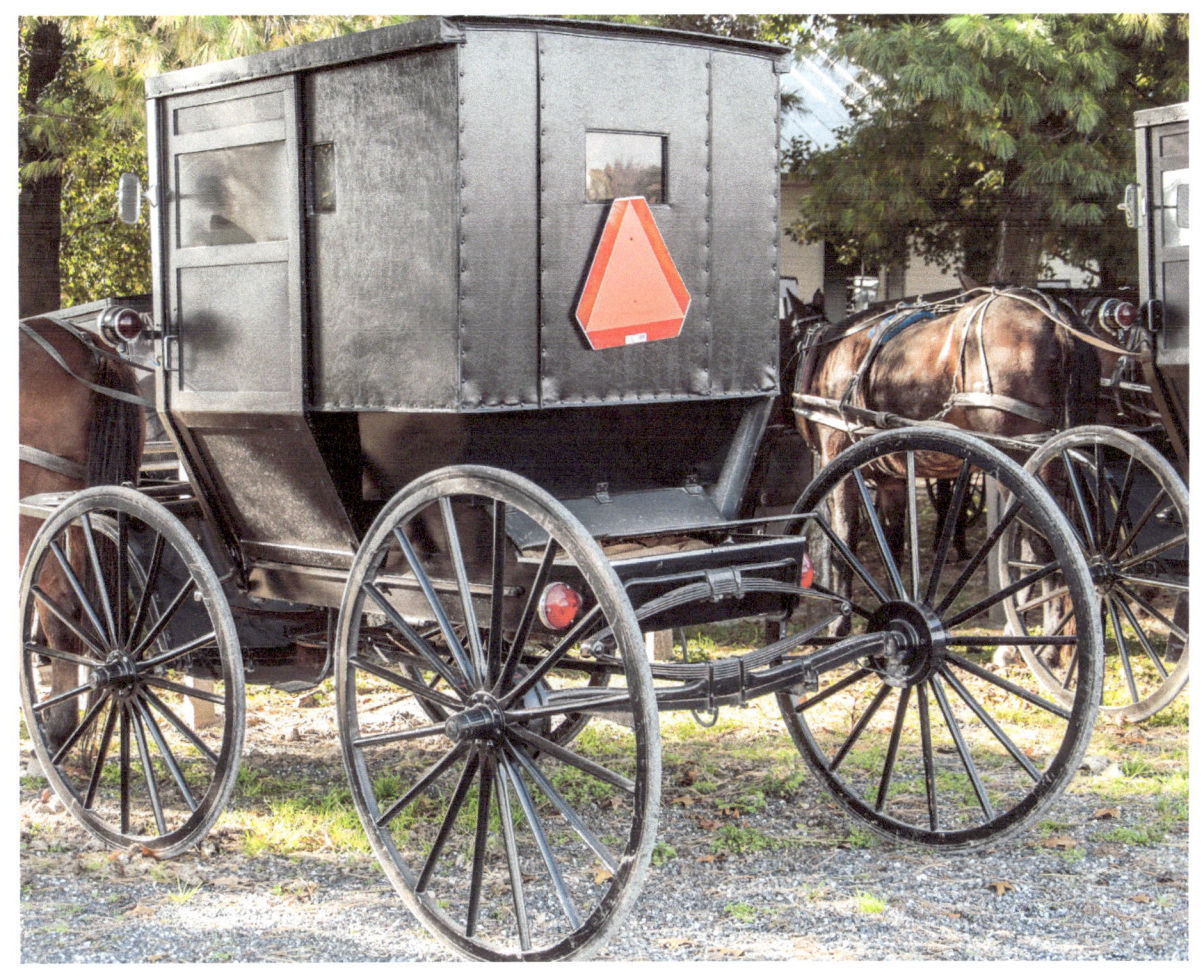

A Wagon akin to Mennonites

Terrell Garage in Unionville, Virginia

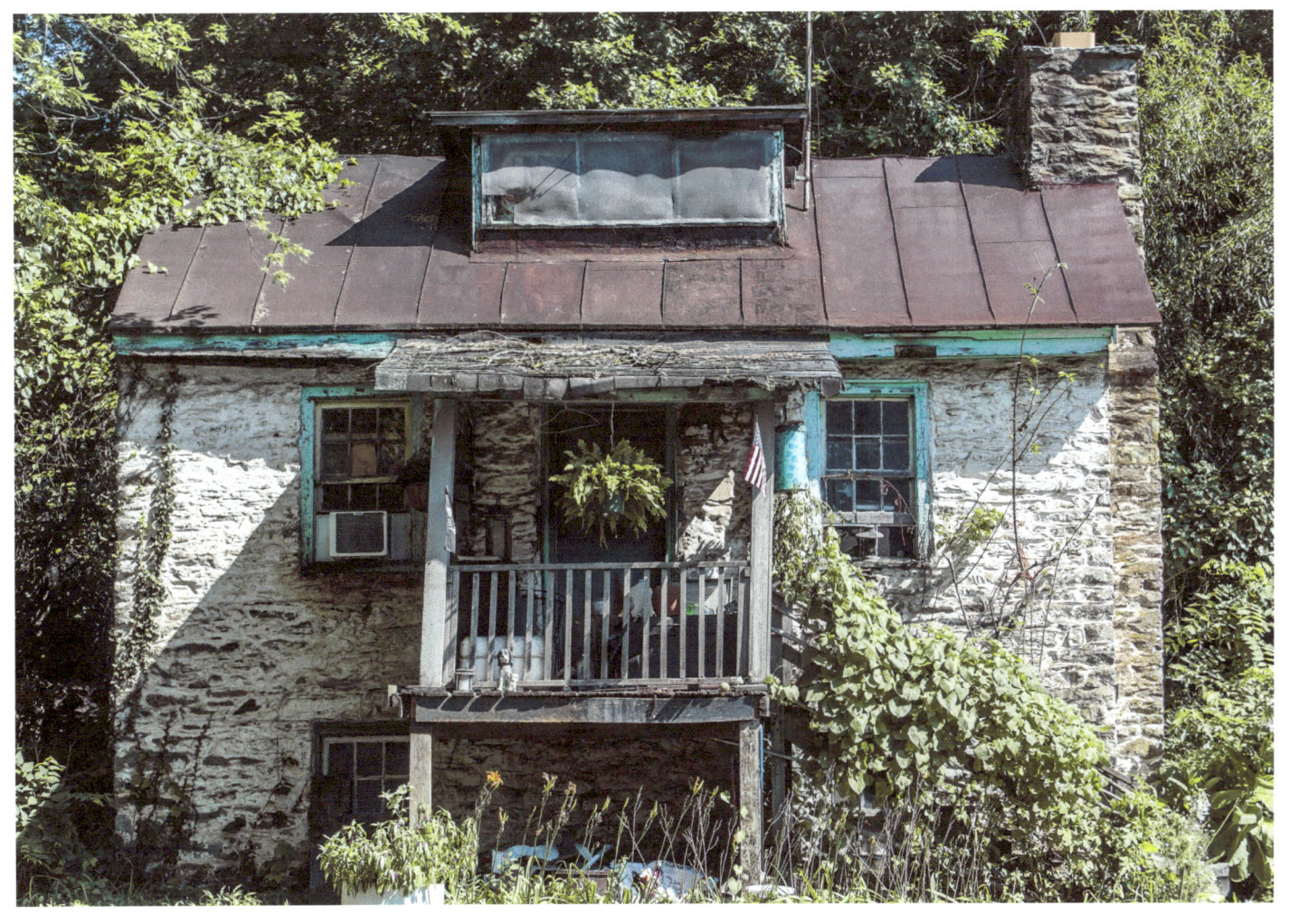

Wayne's Home in Middleburg, Virginia

Historic House in Petersburg, Virginia

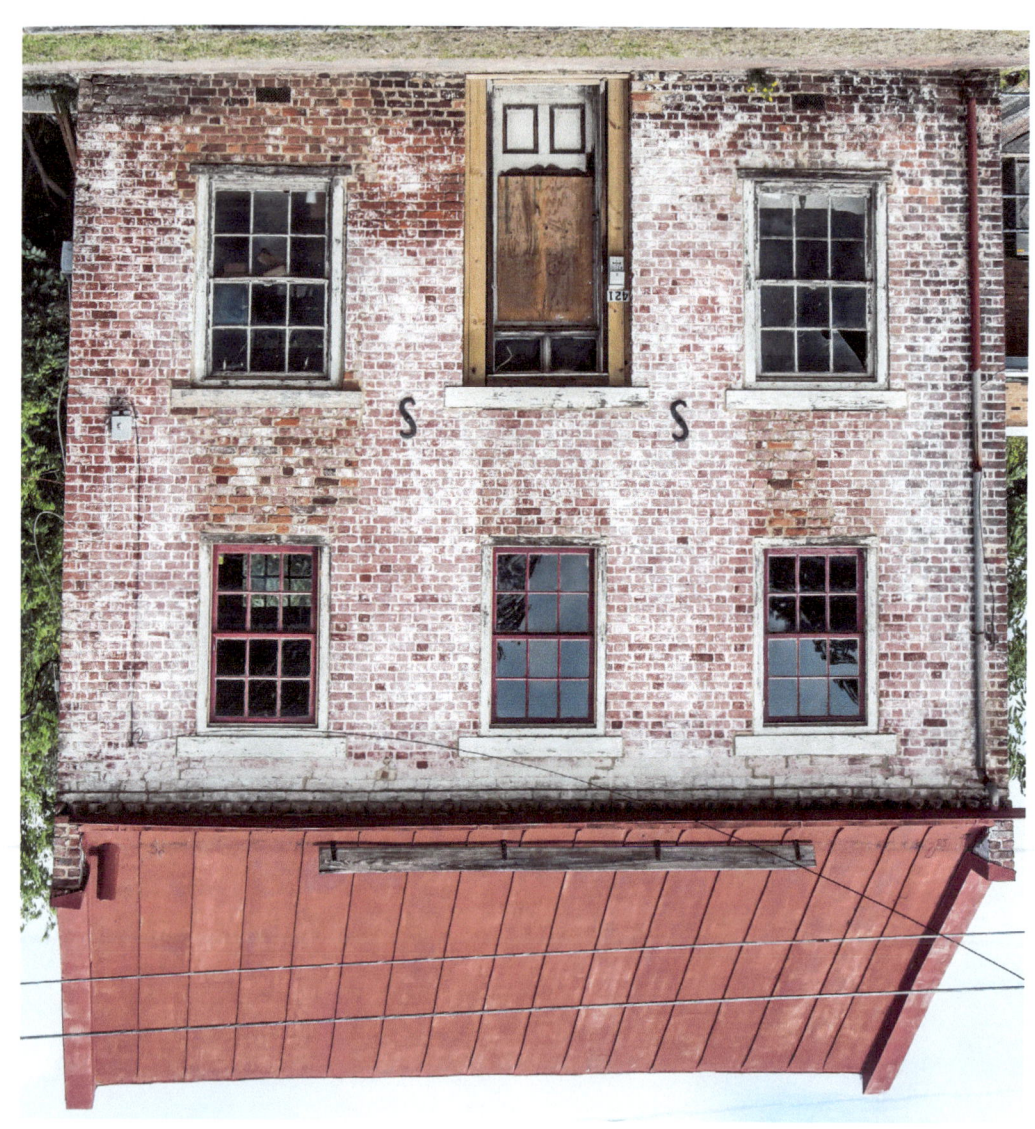

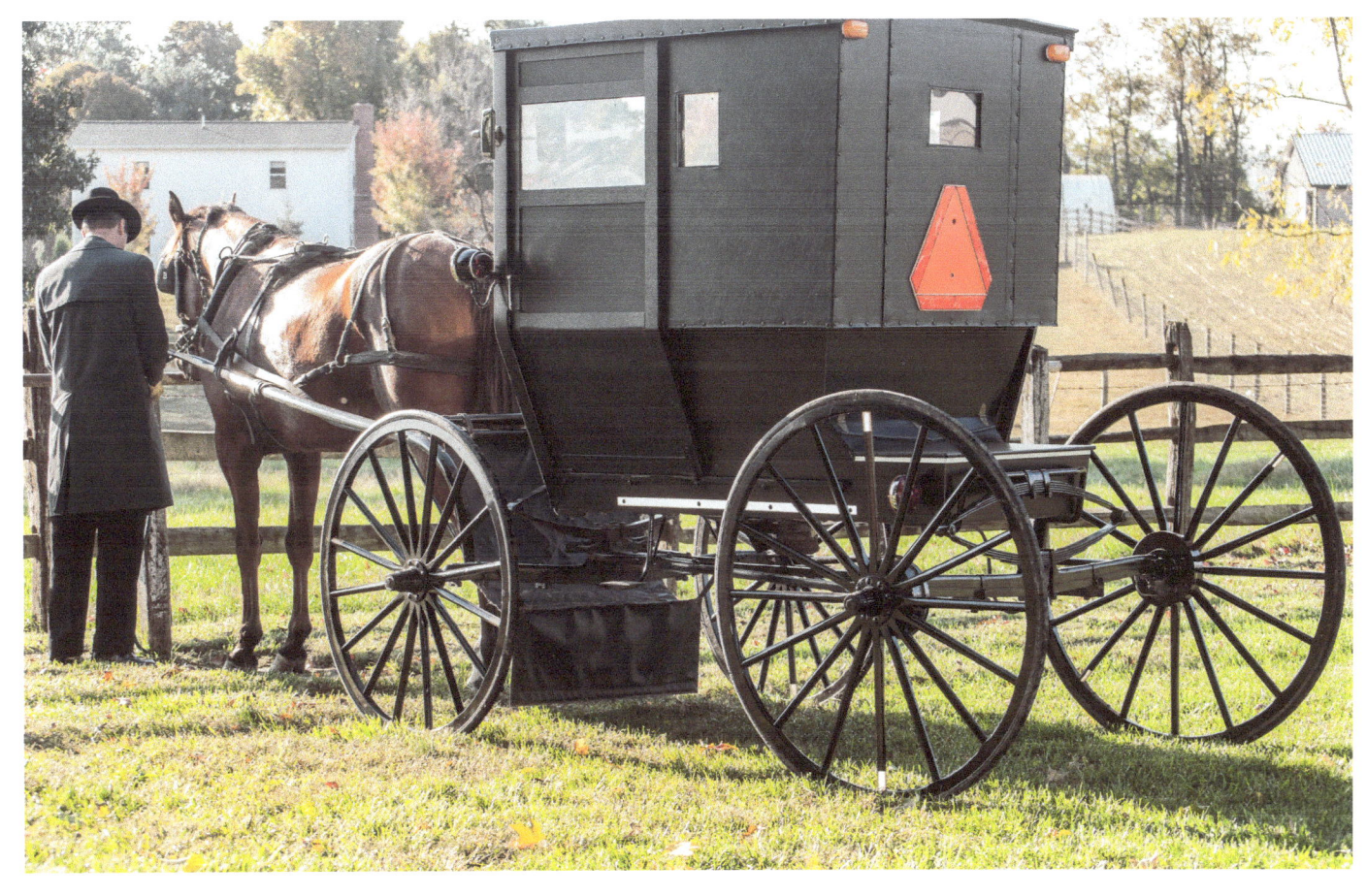

Early Arrival in a Black Wood-Framed Buggy

1927 Model T Speedster

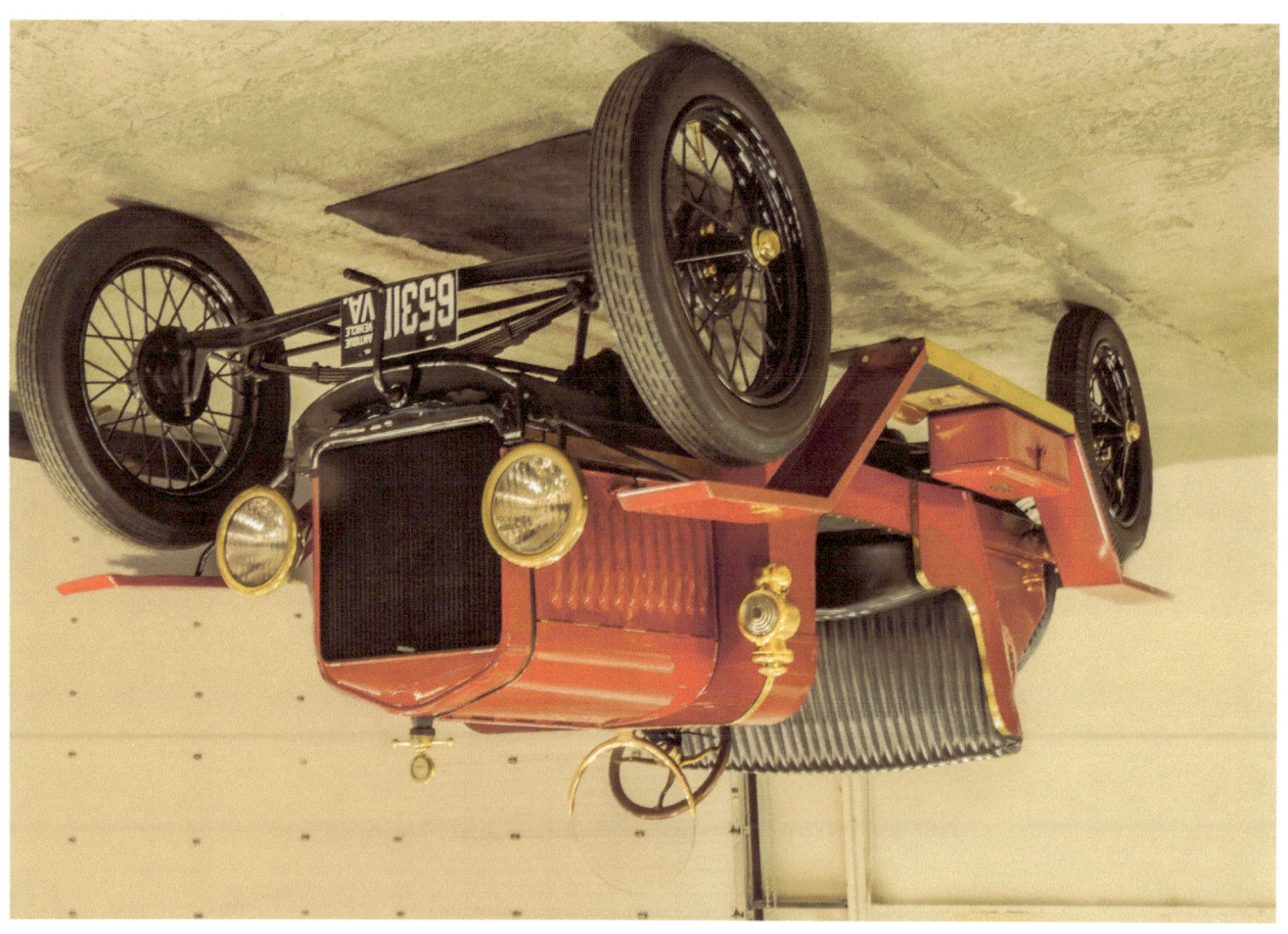

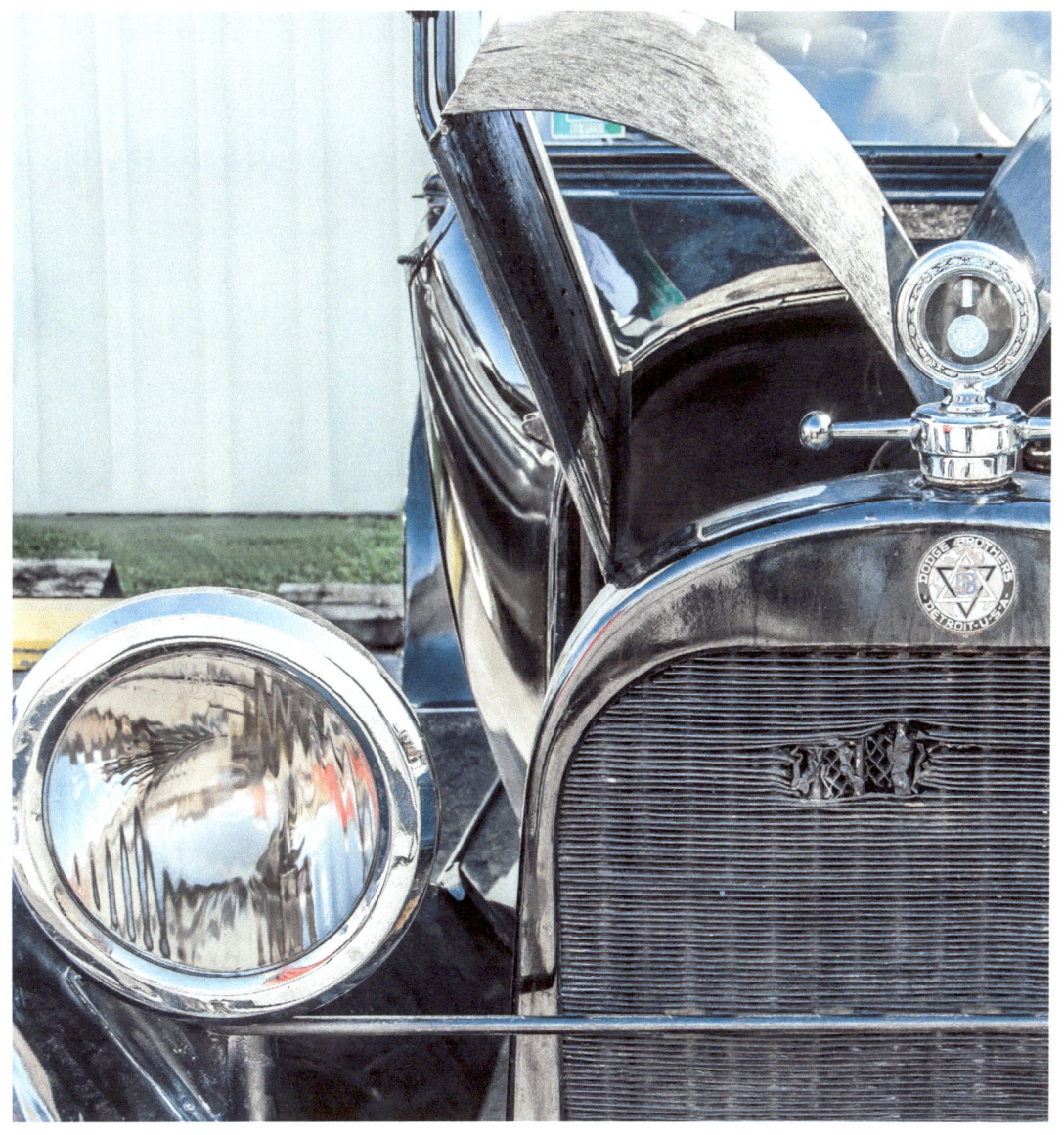

1921 Dodge Brothers Touring Car

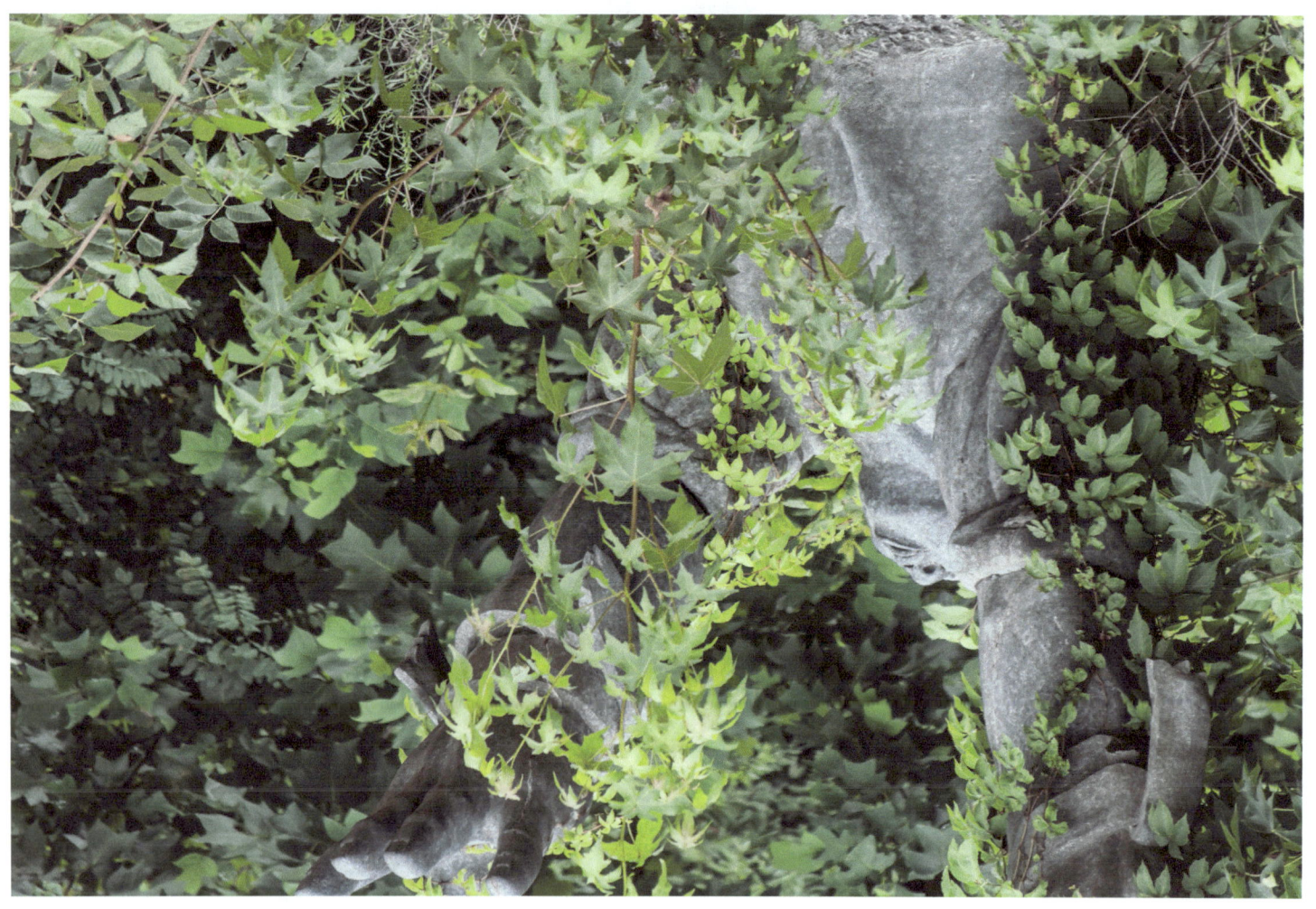

A Ruin from the Proposed United States National Slavery Museum in Fredericksburg, Virginia

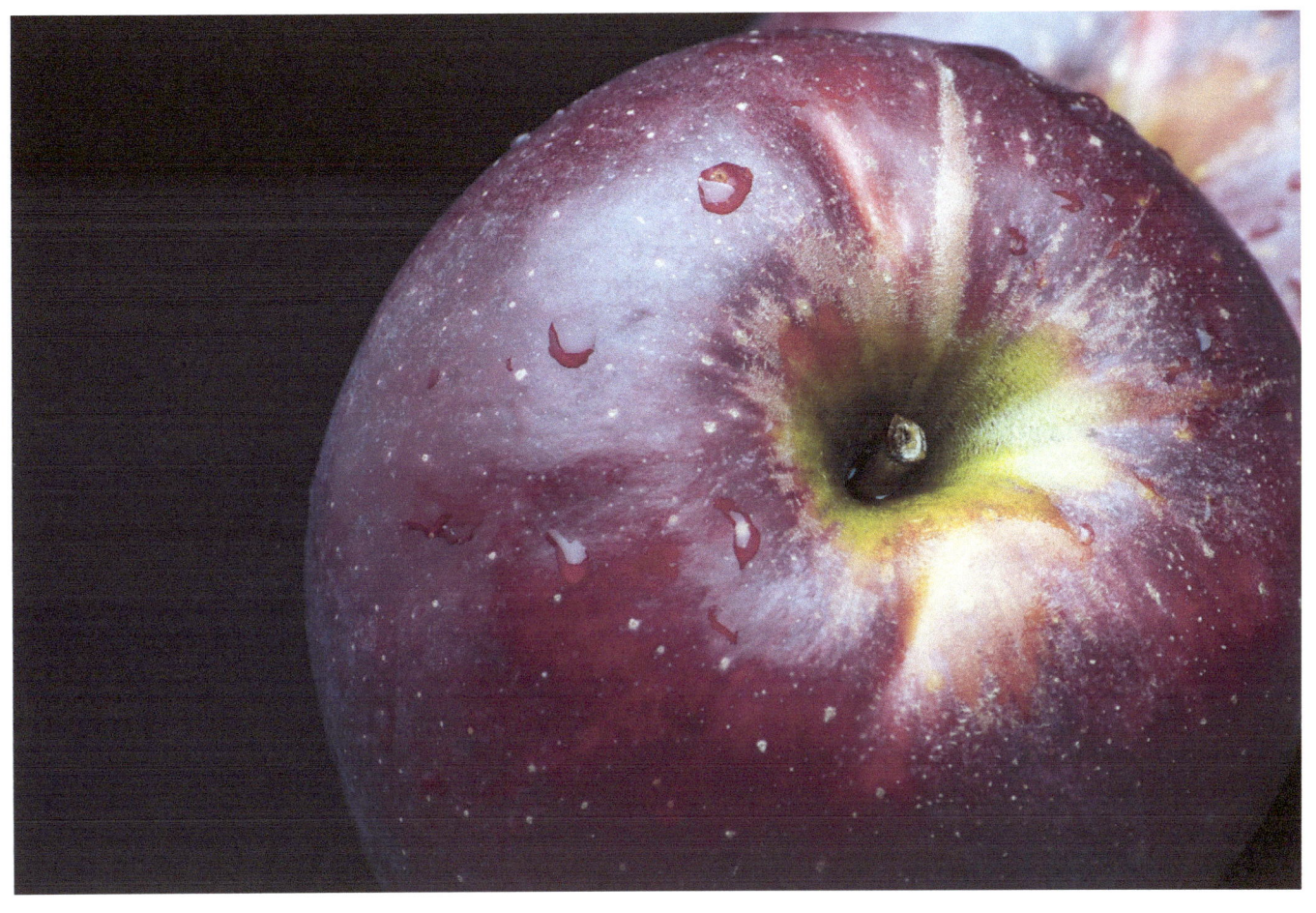

Apple Country - The Northern Shenandoah Valley

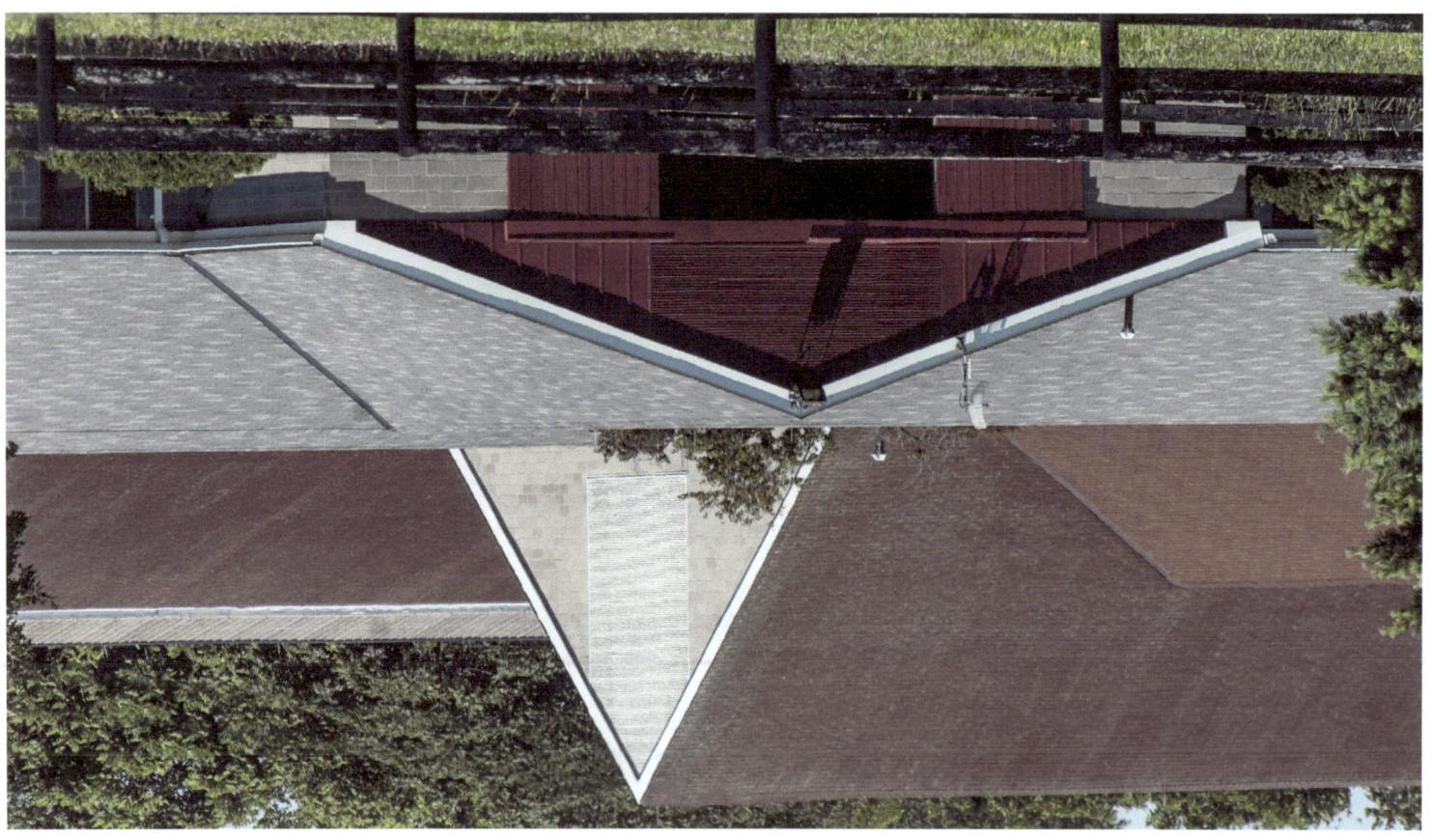

Barn Complex, Foxcroft School in Middleburg, Virginia

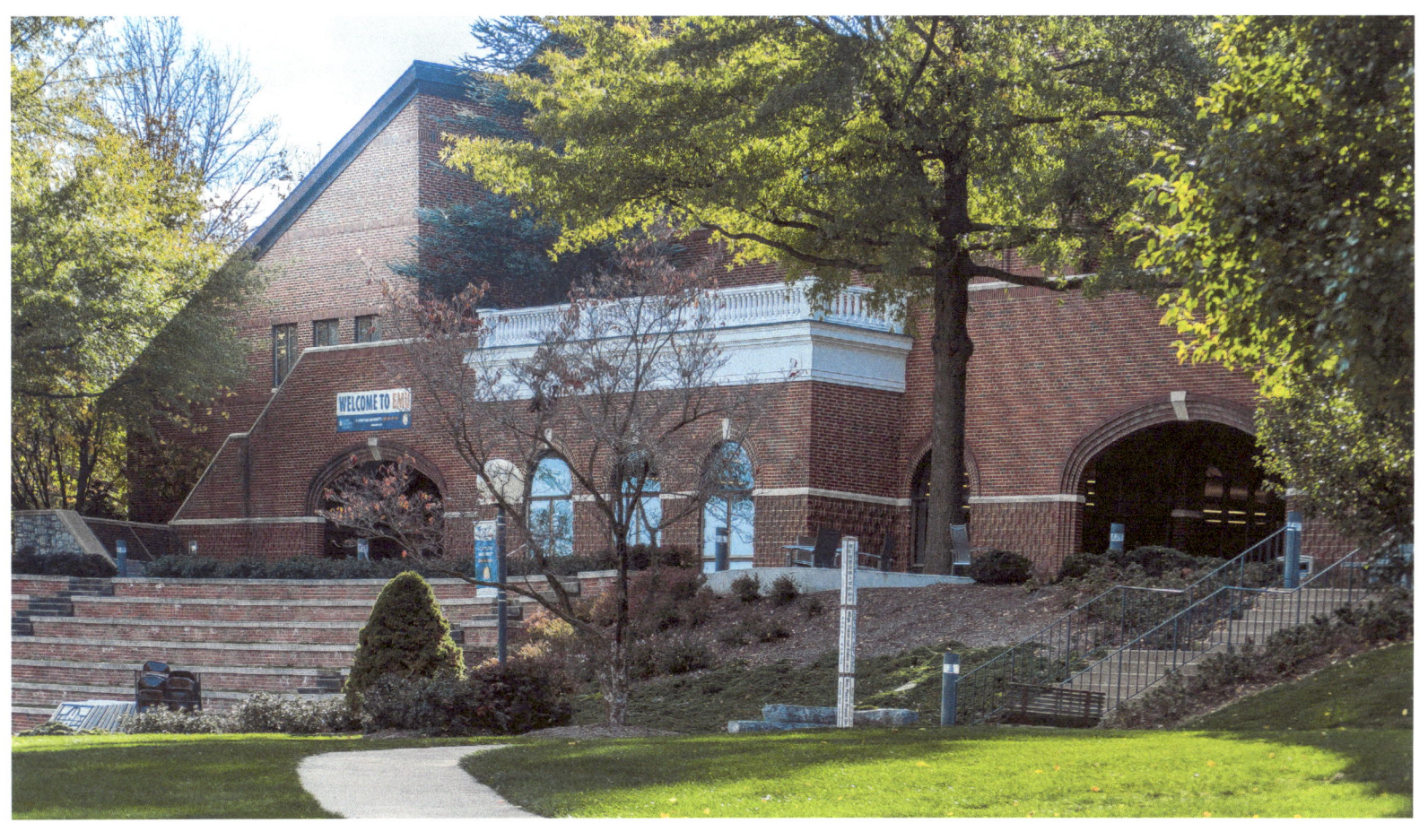

Eastern Mennonite University in Harrisonburg, Virginia

Colorful Tower Silos on Farm in Dayton, Virginia

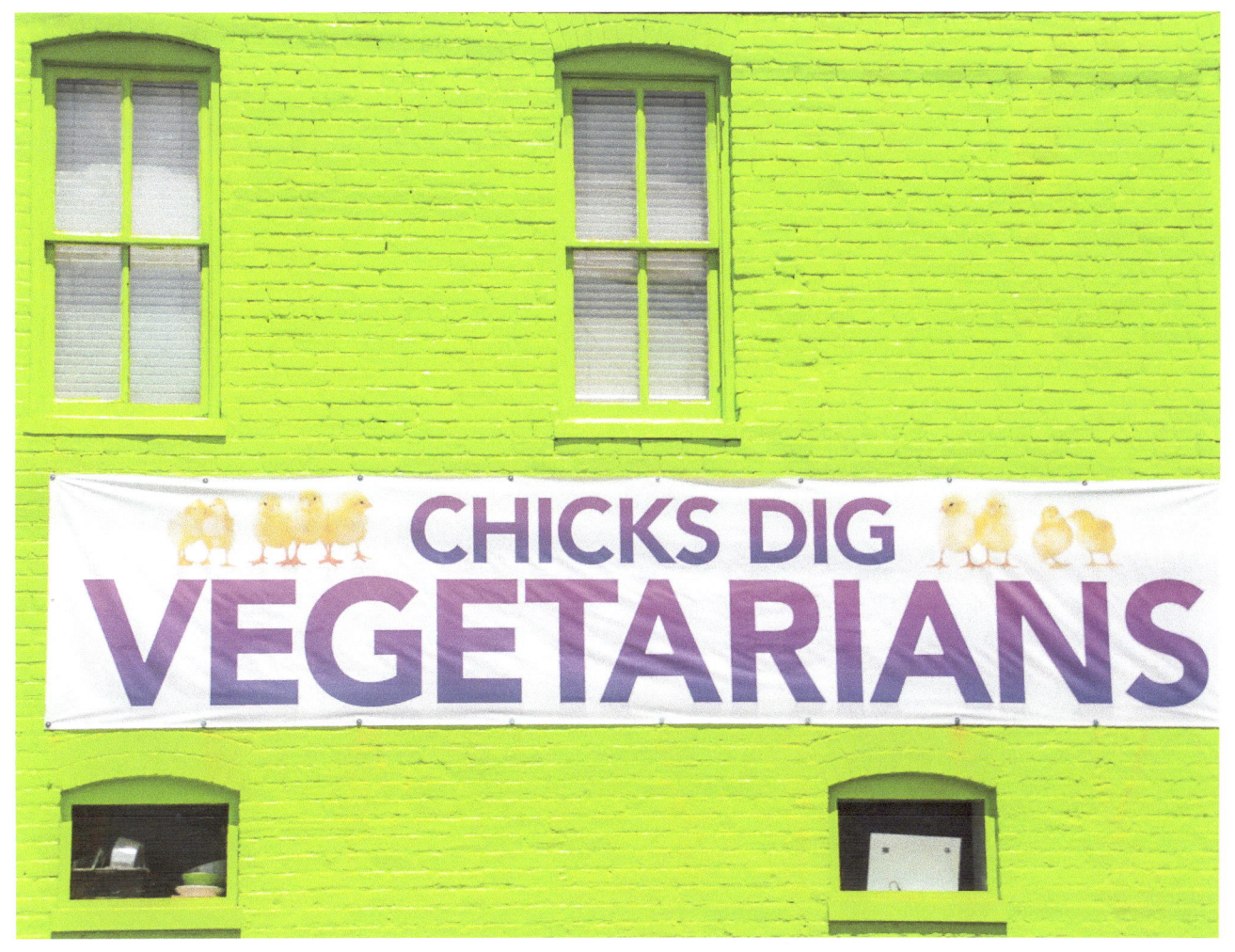

Eatery Sign "Chicks Dig Vegetarians"

Maggie Lena Walker's St. Luke Penny Savings Bankbook

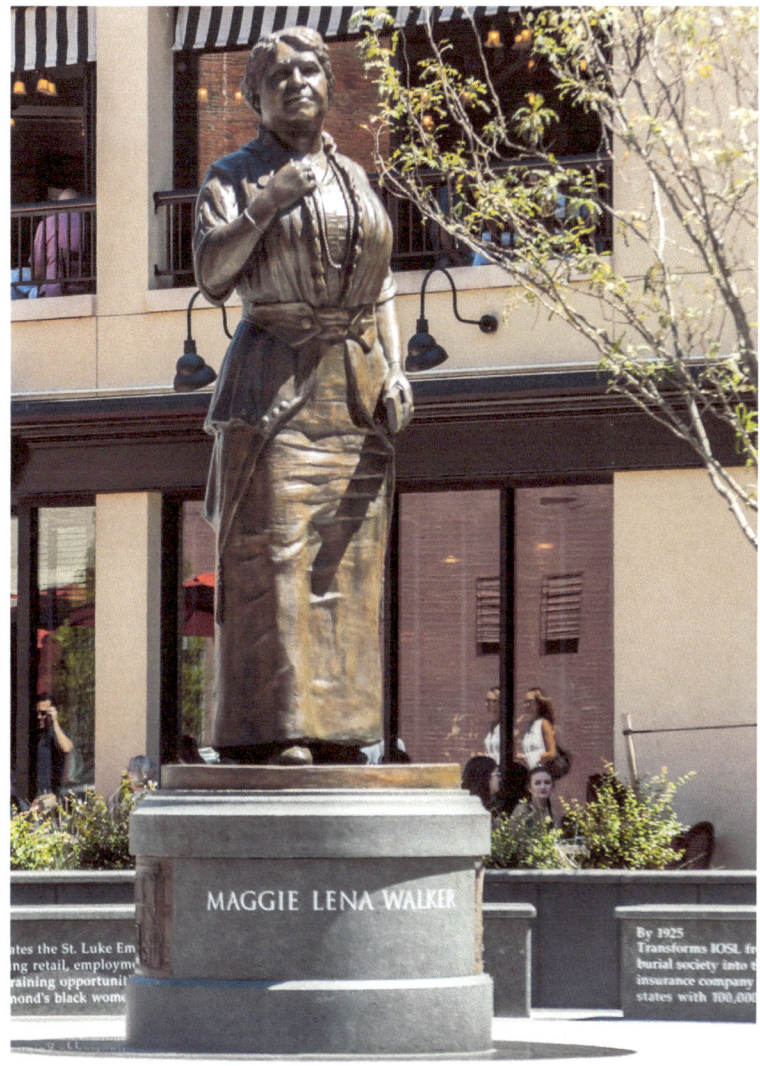

The Maggie L. Walker Monument in Richmond, Virginia

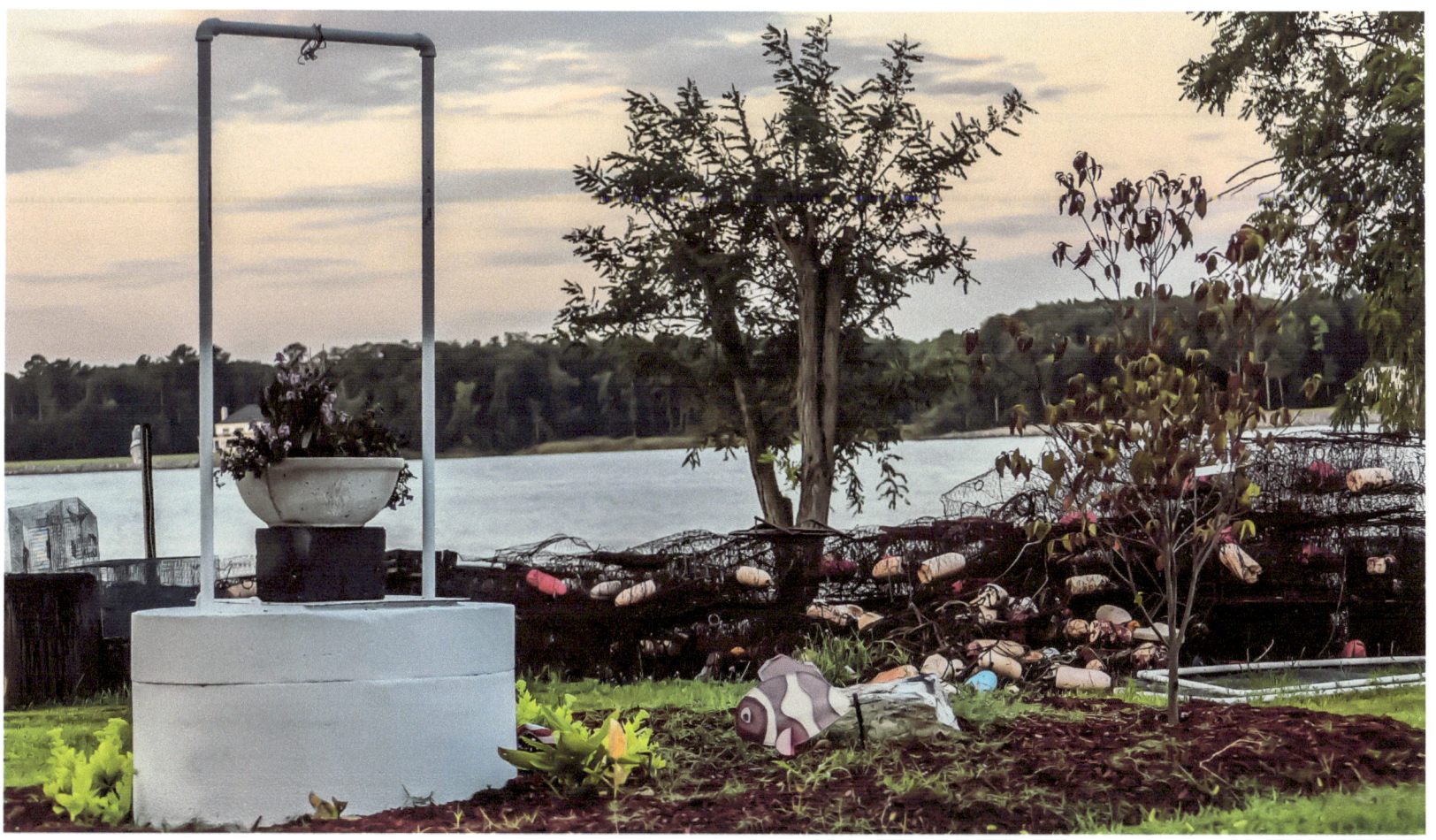

Waterfront View from Friends' Summer Home in Sandy Point, Virginia

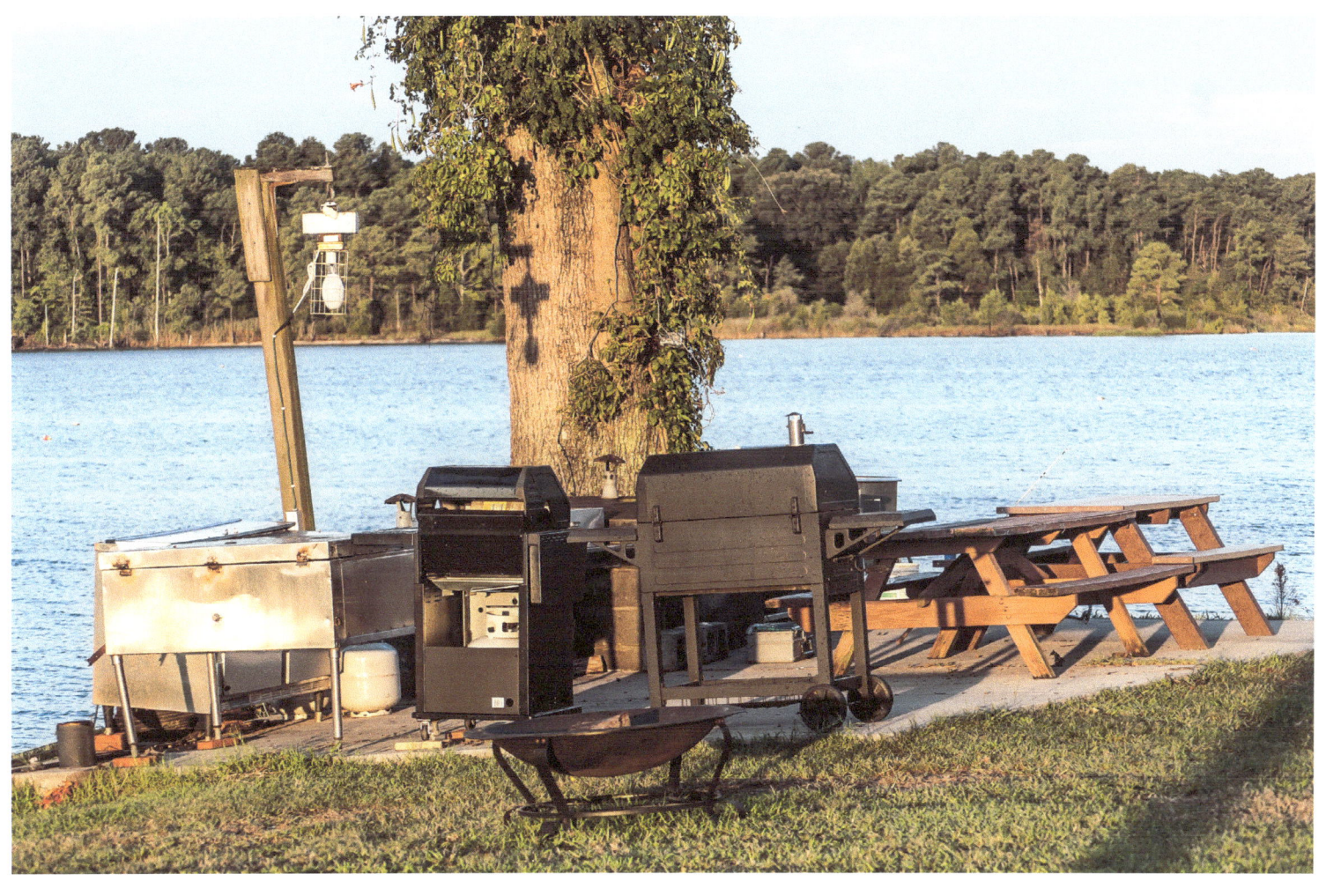

Quality of Light Image in Sandy Point, Virginia

The Arthur Robert Ashe, Jr. Monument in Richmond, Virginia

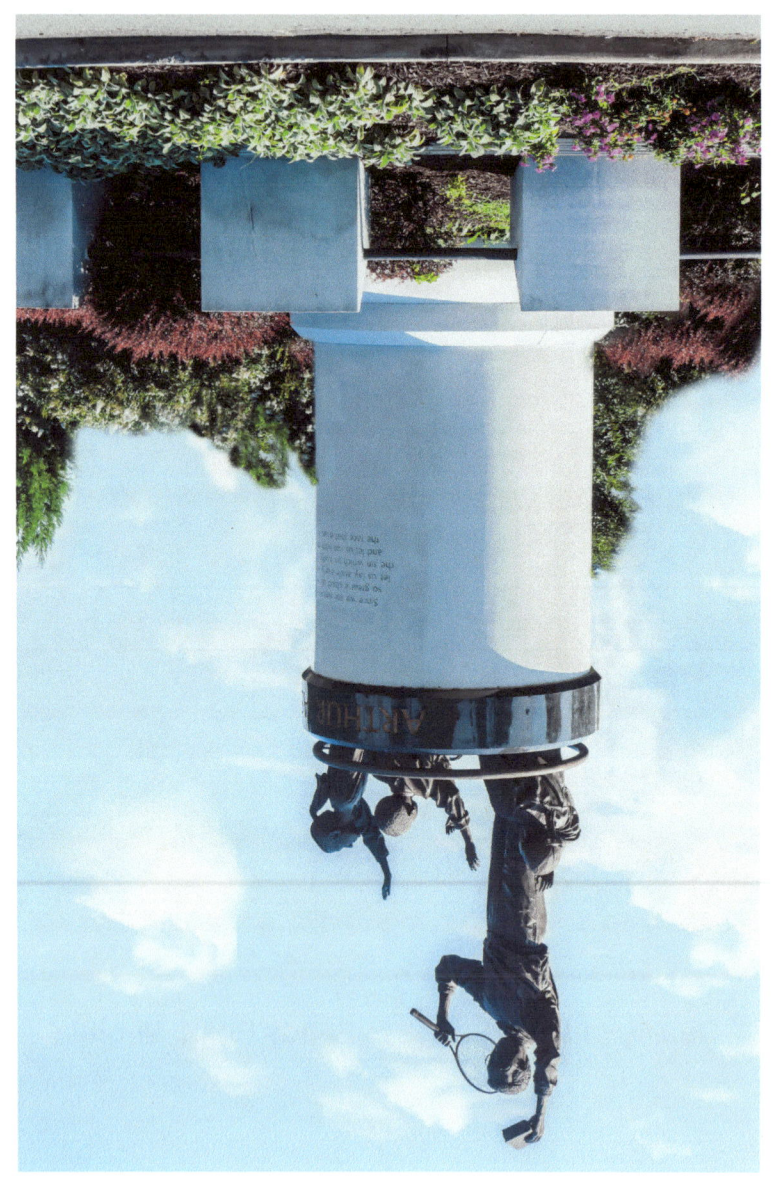

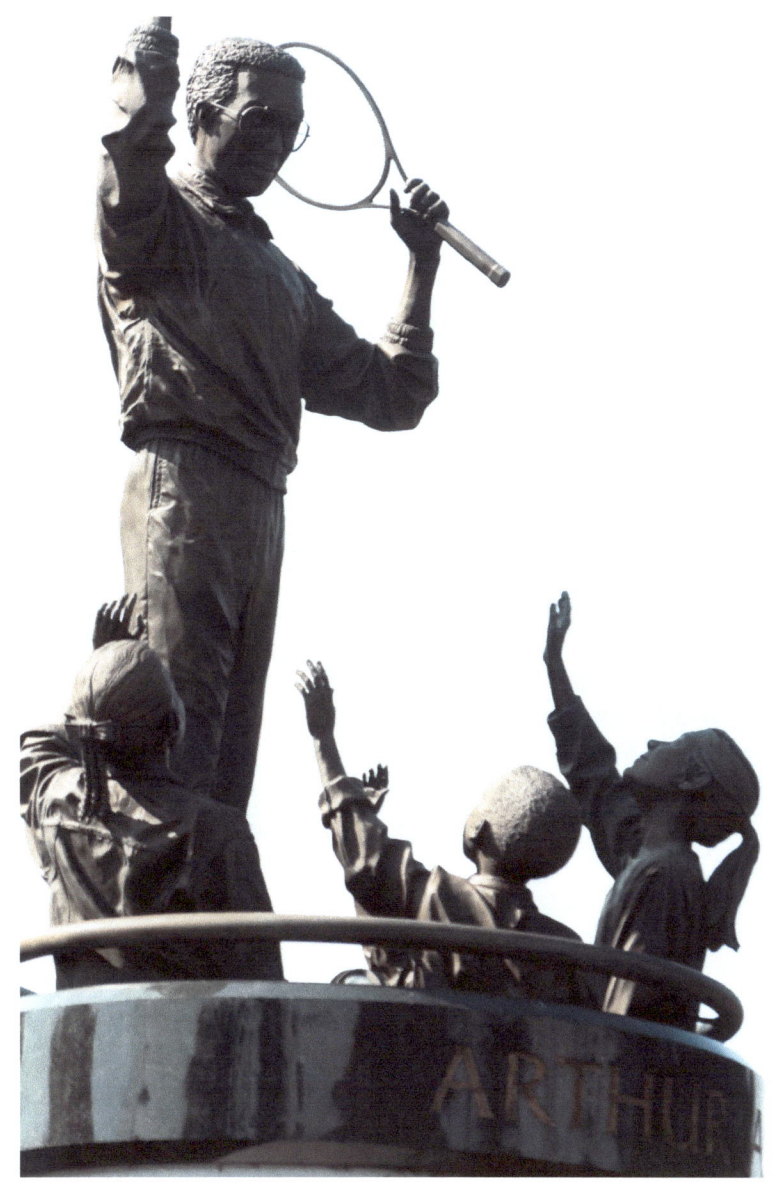

Arthur Robert Ashe, Jr., Professional Tennis Player from Richmond, Virginia

James Madison University in Harrisonburg, Virginia

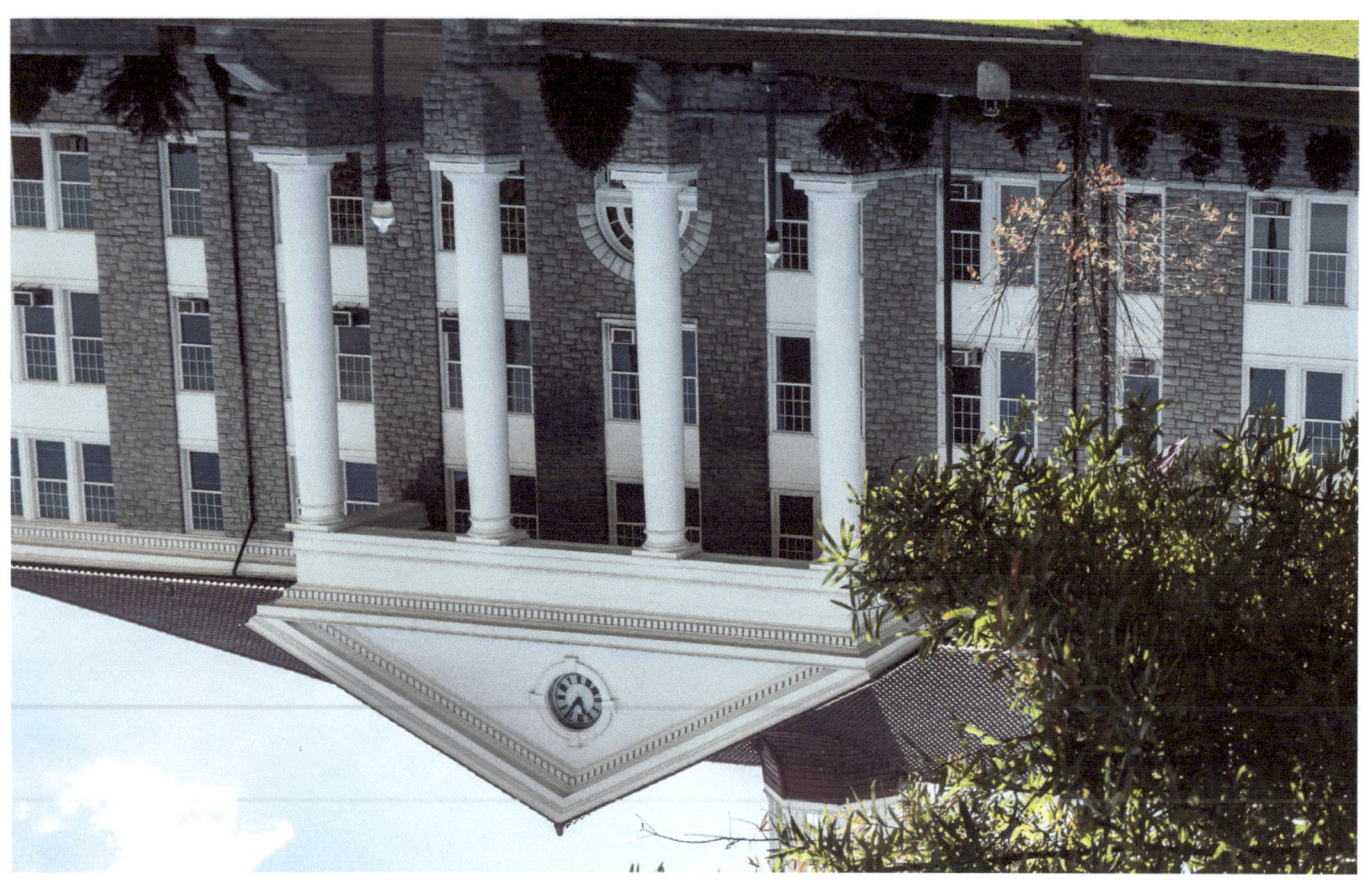

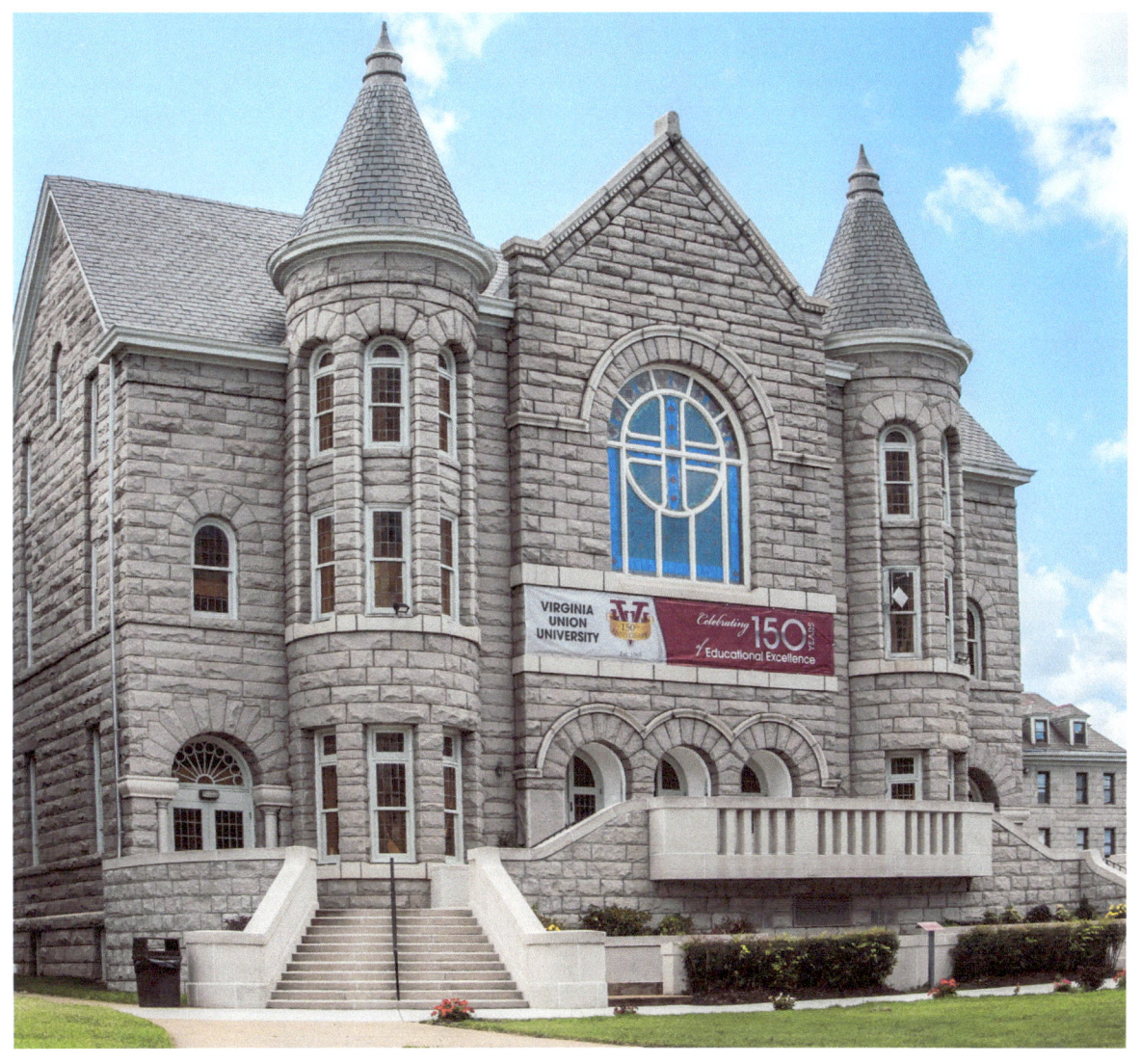

Virginia Union University in Richmond, Virginia

Rumors of War in front of the Virginia Museum of Fine Arts

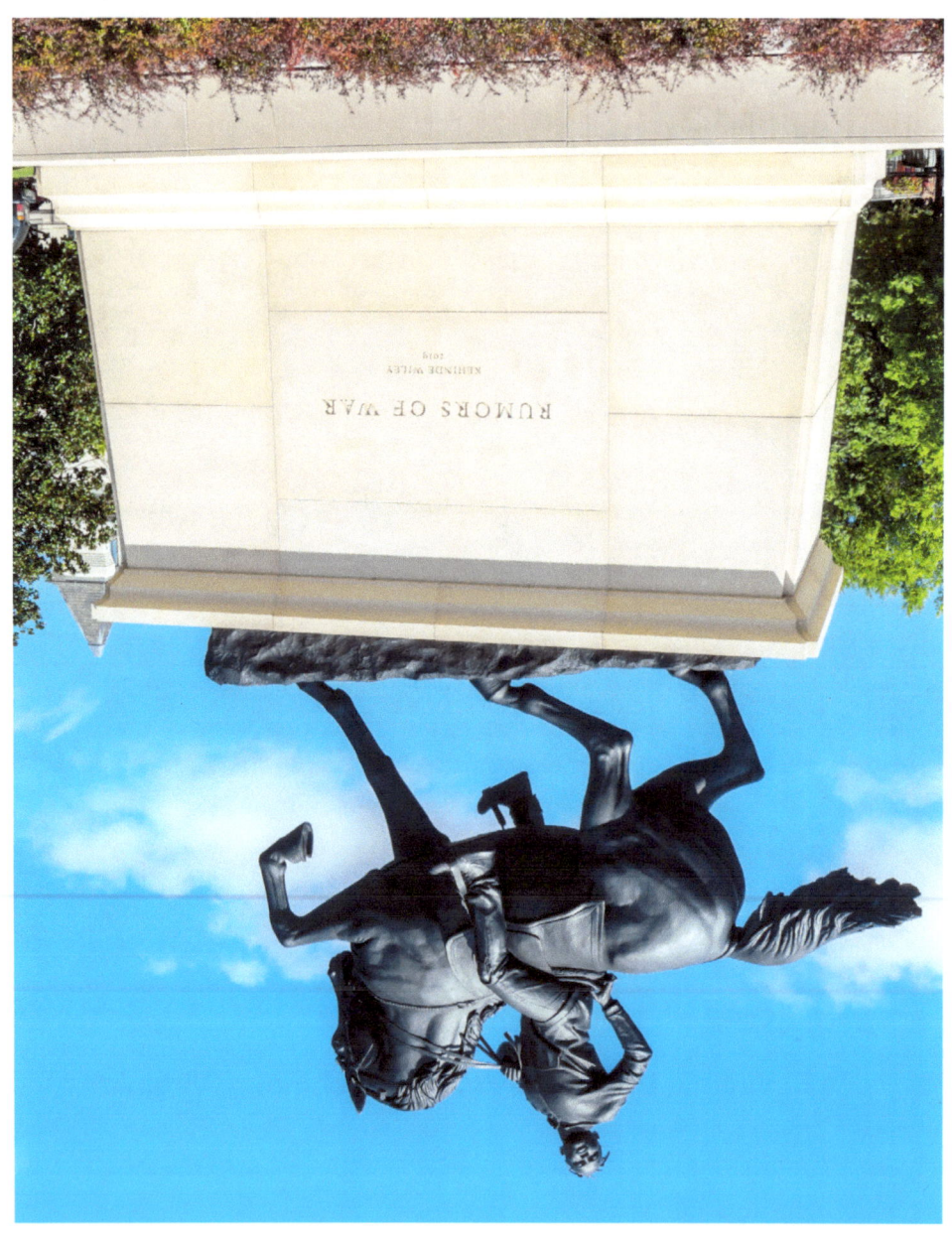

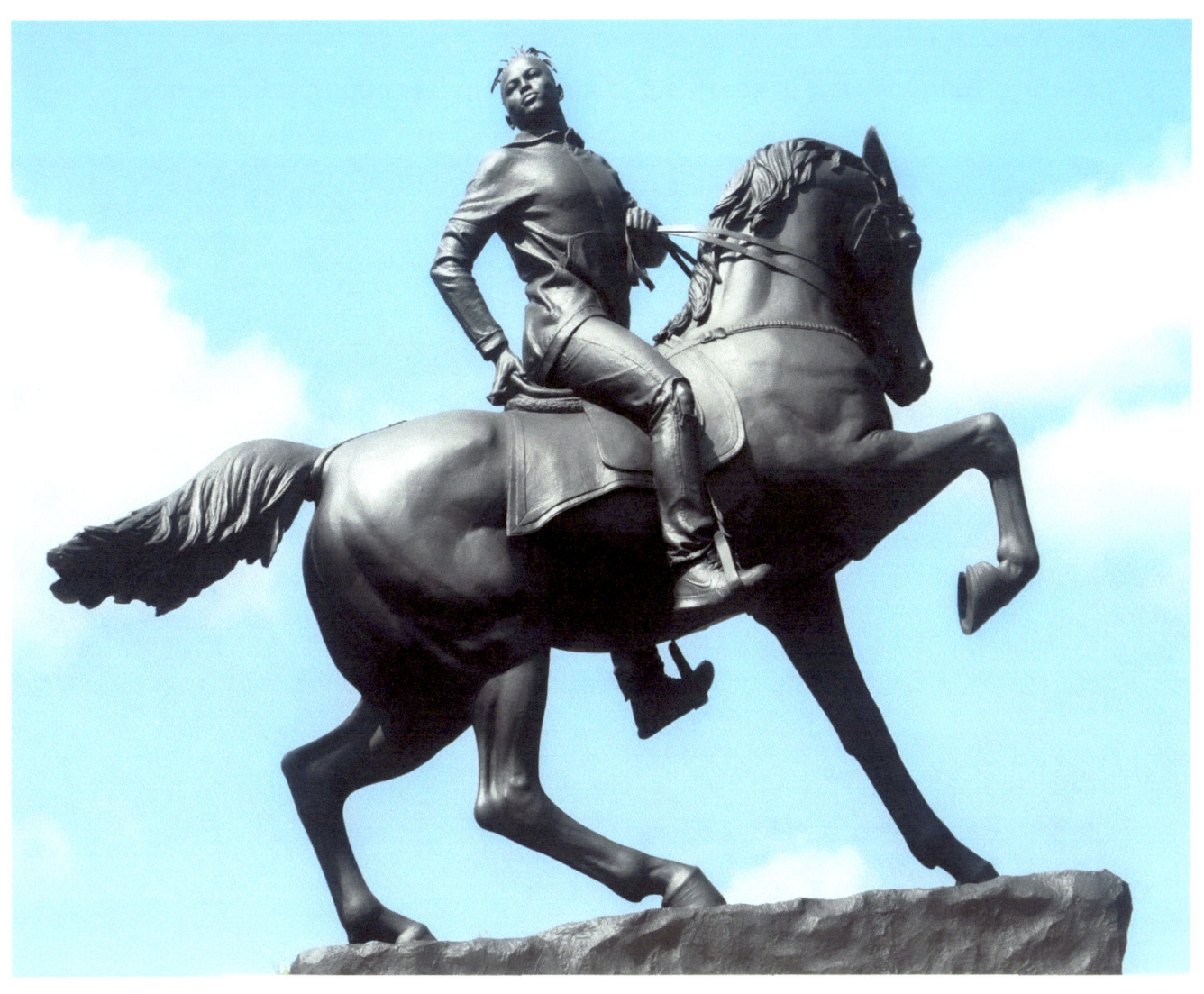

Rumors of War by Kehinde Wiley

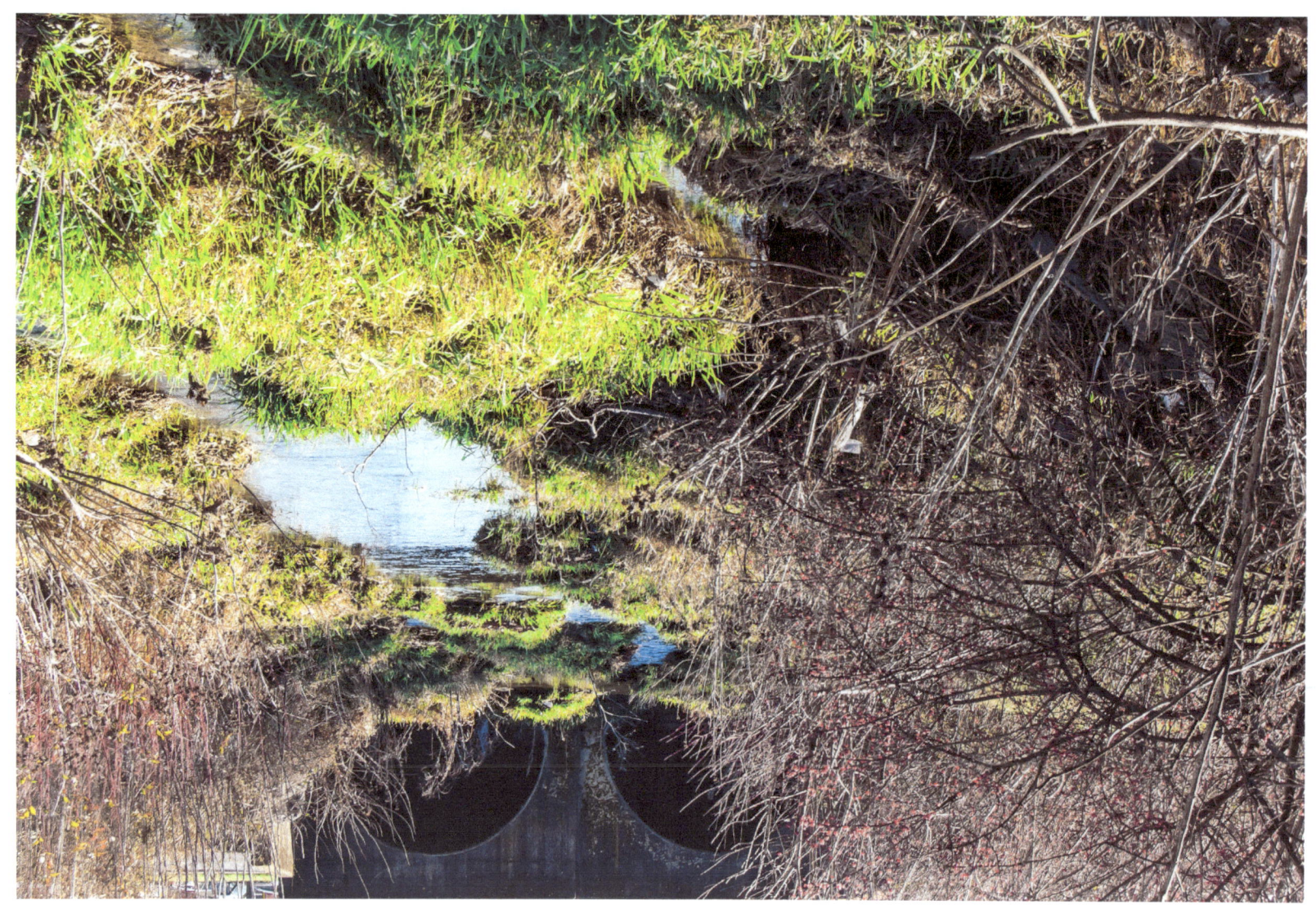

Double Arch Bridge and the Beauty of the Creek in Harrisonburg, Virginia

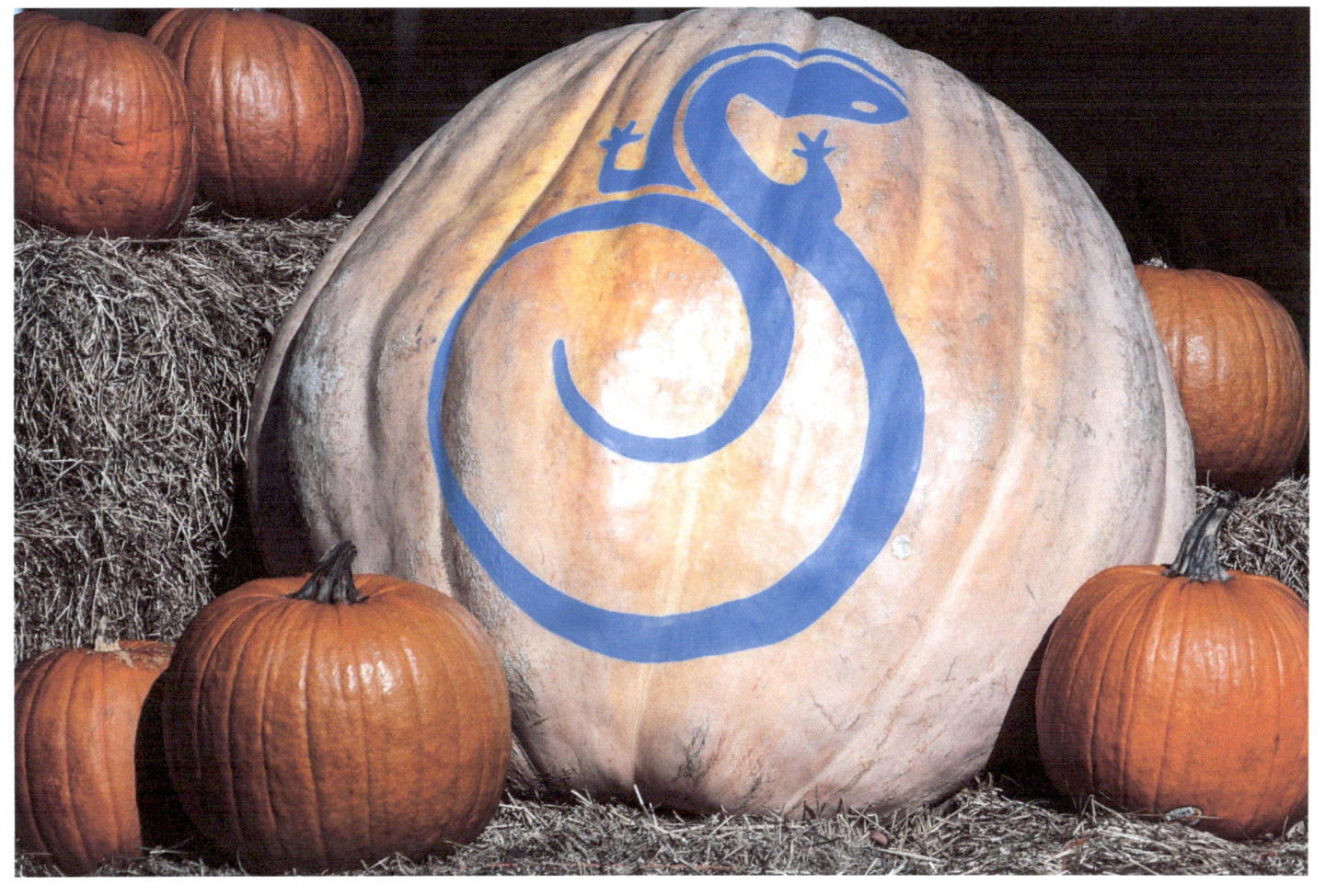

A Welcoming Pumpkin During Thanksgiving at Salamander Resort & Spa, in Middleburg, Virginia

Statue of Door at Clay Street Playground in Richmond, Virginia

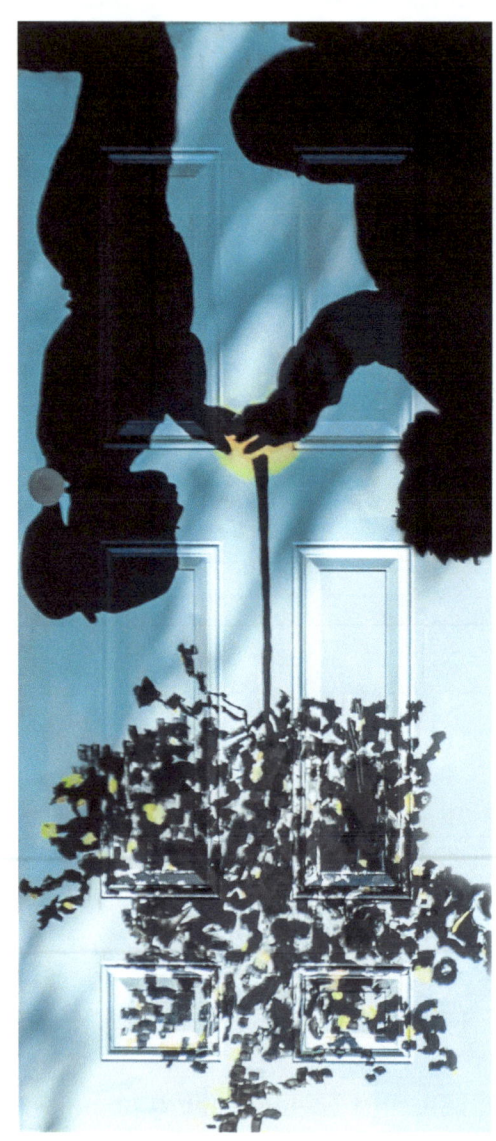

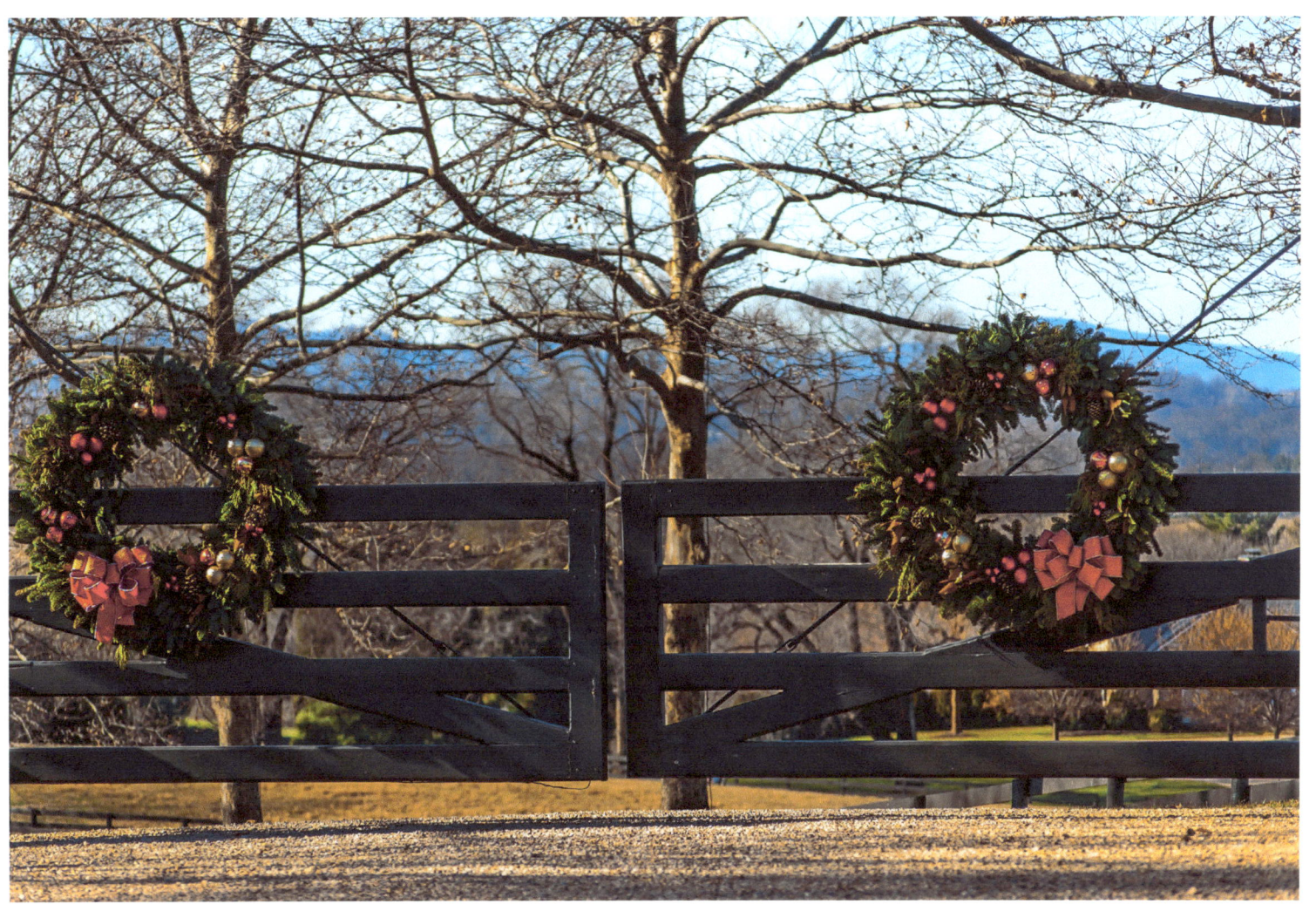

"A View from Afar" at Christmastime in Middleburg, Virginia

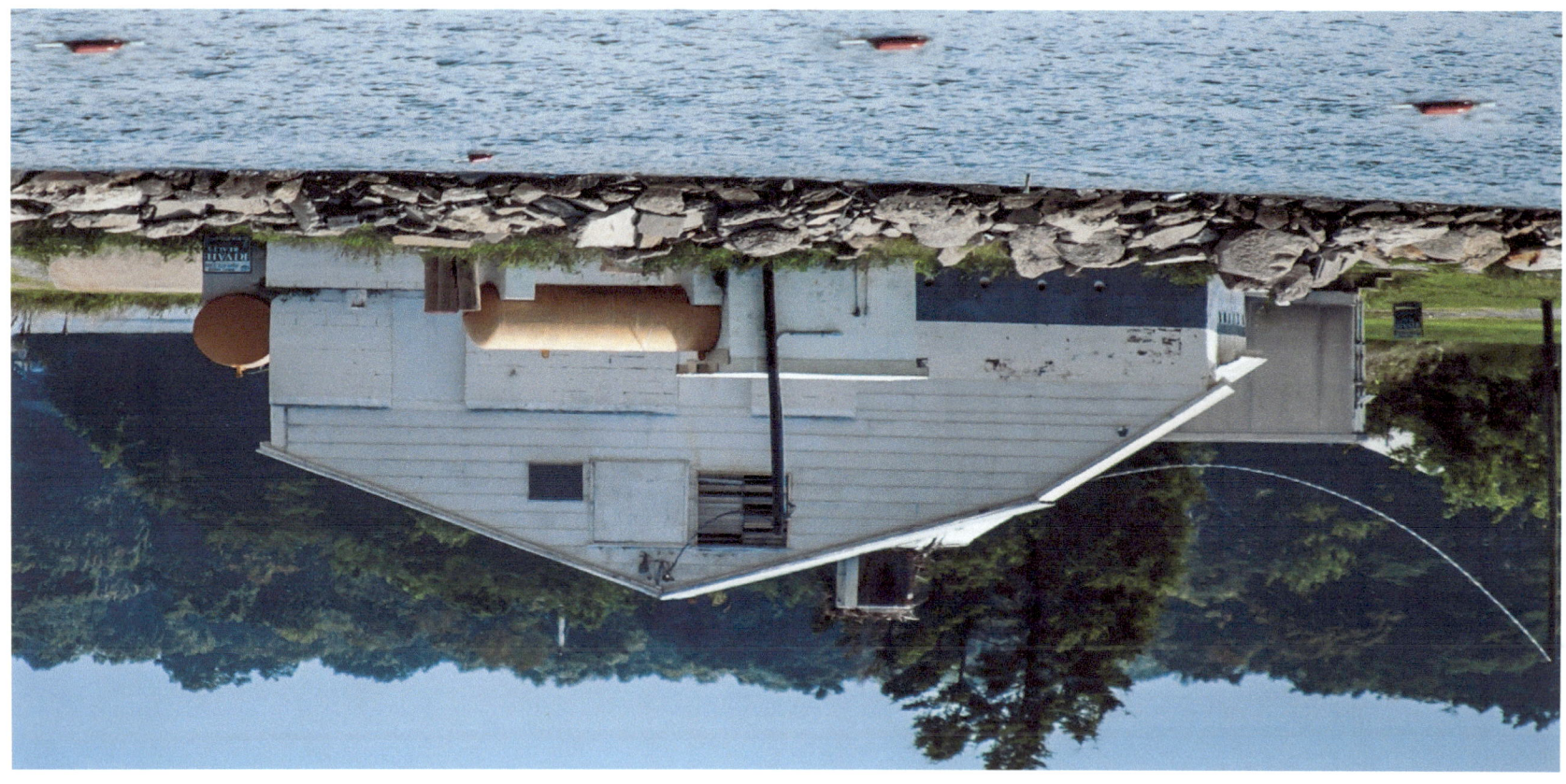

A Crab House in Sandy Point, Virginia

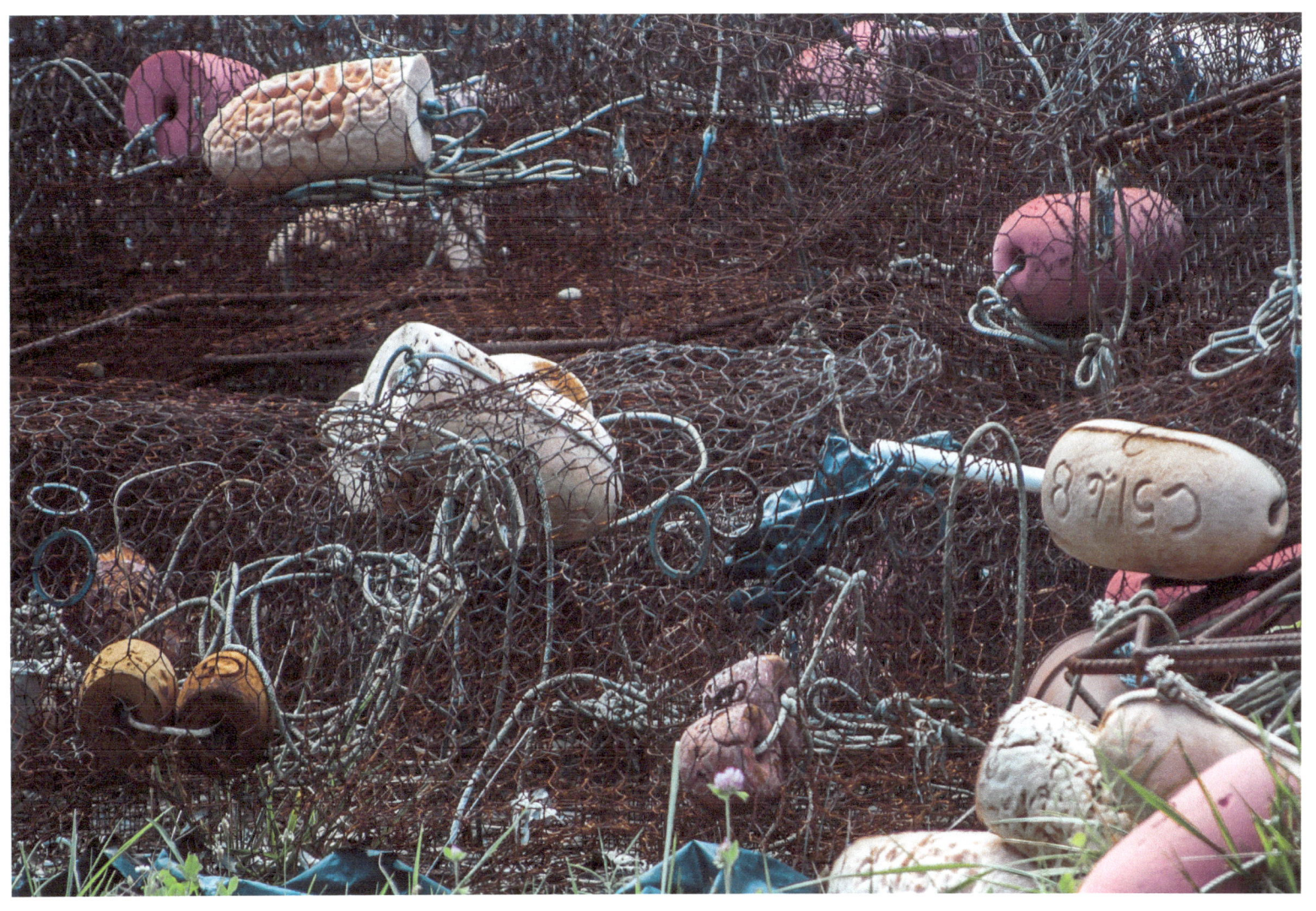

Colorful Buoys in Sandy Point, Virginia

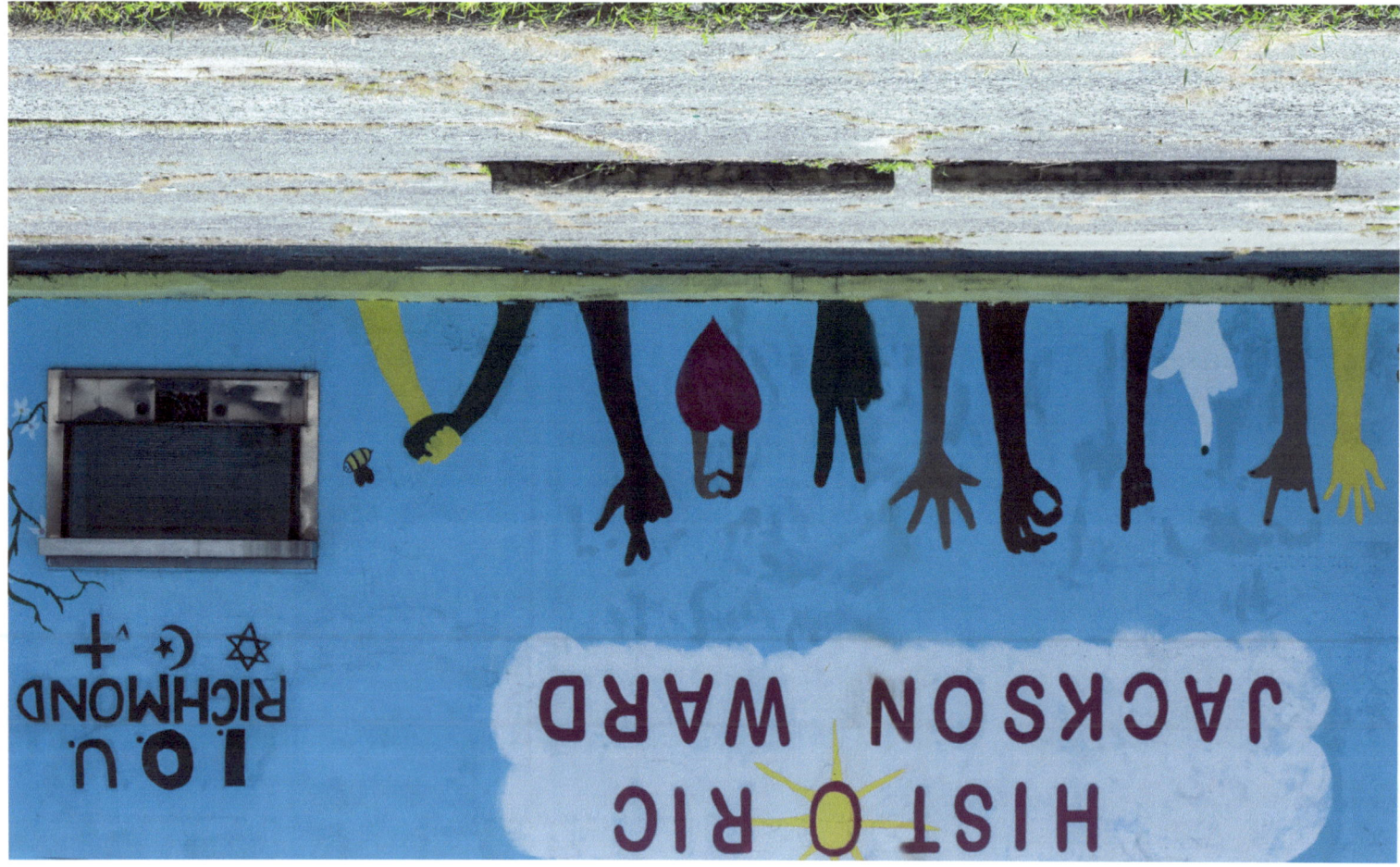

Historic Jackson Ward in Richmond, Virginia

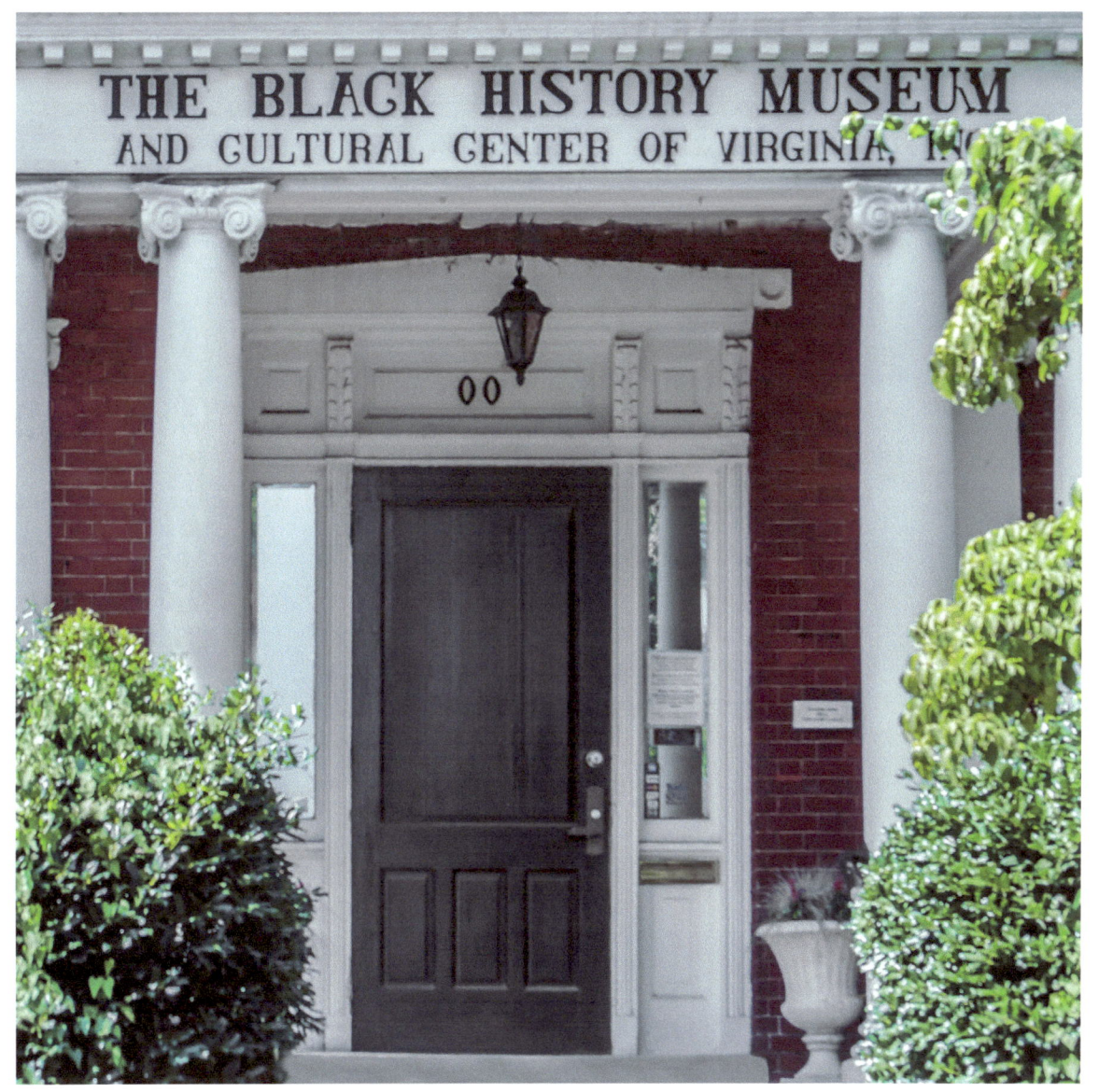

The Black History Museum of Virginia in Richmond, Virginia

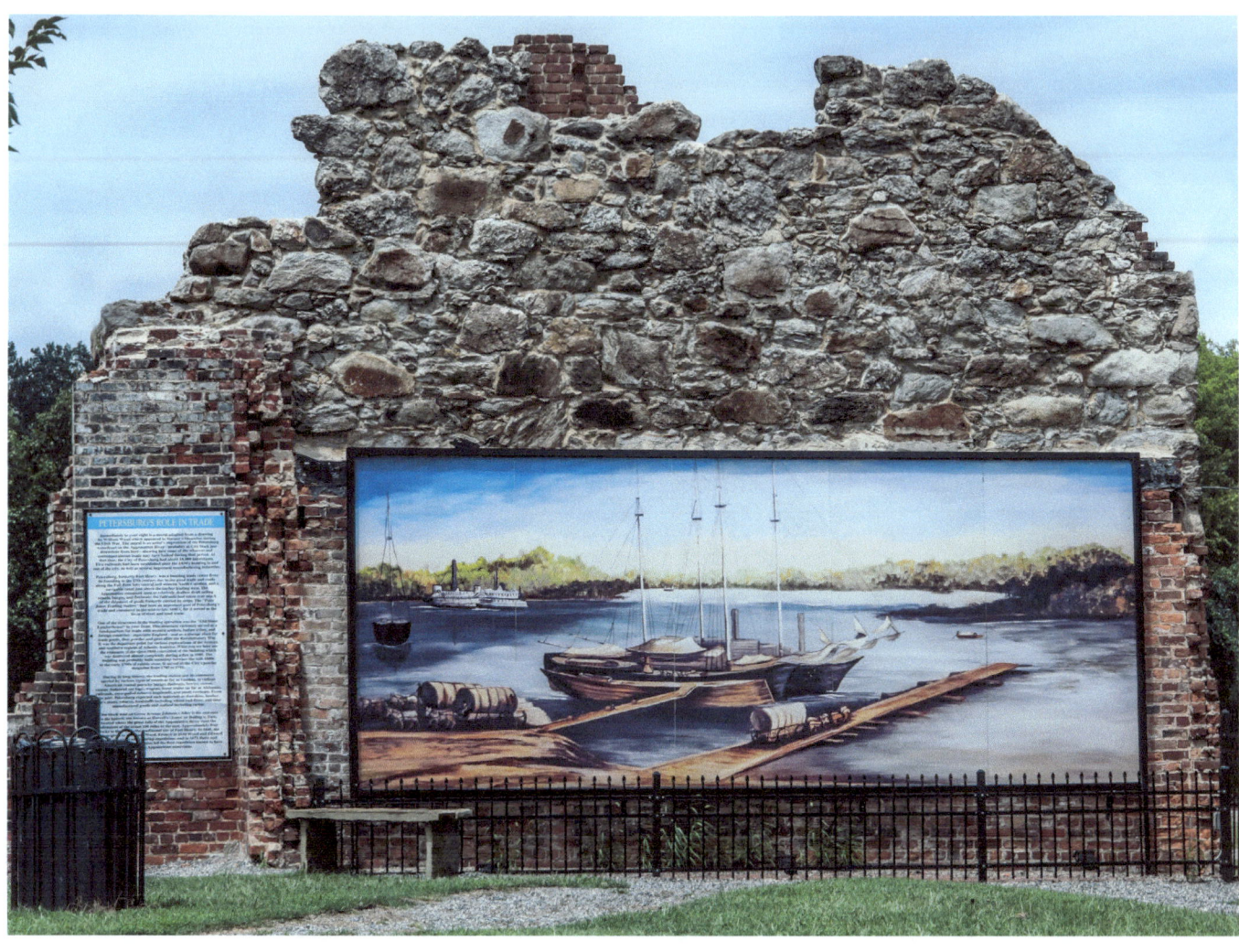

Artist's Impression of the Petersburg Waterfront on the Appomattox River (Civil War)

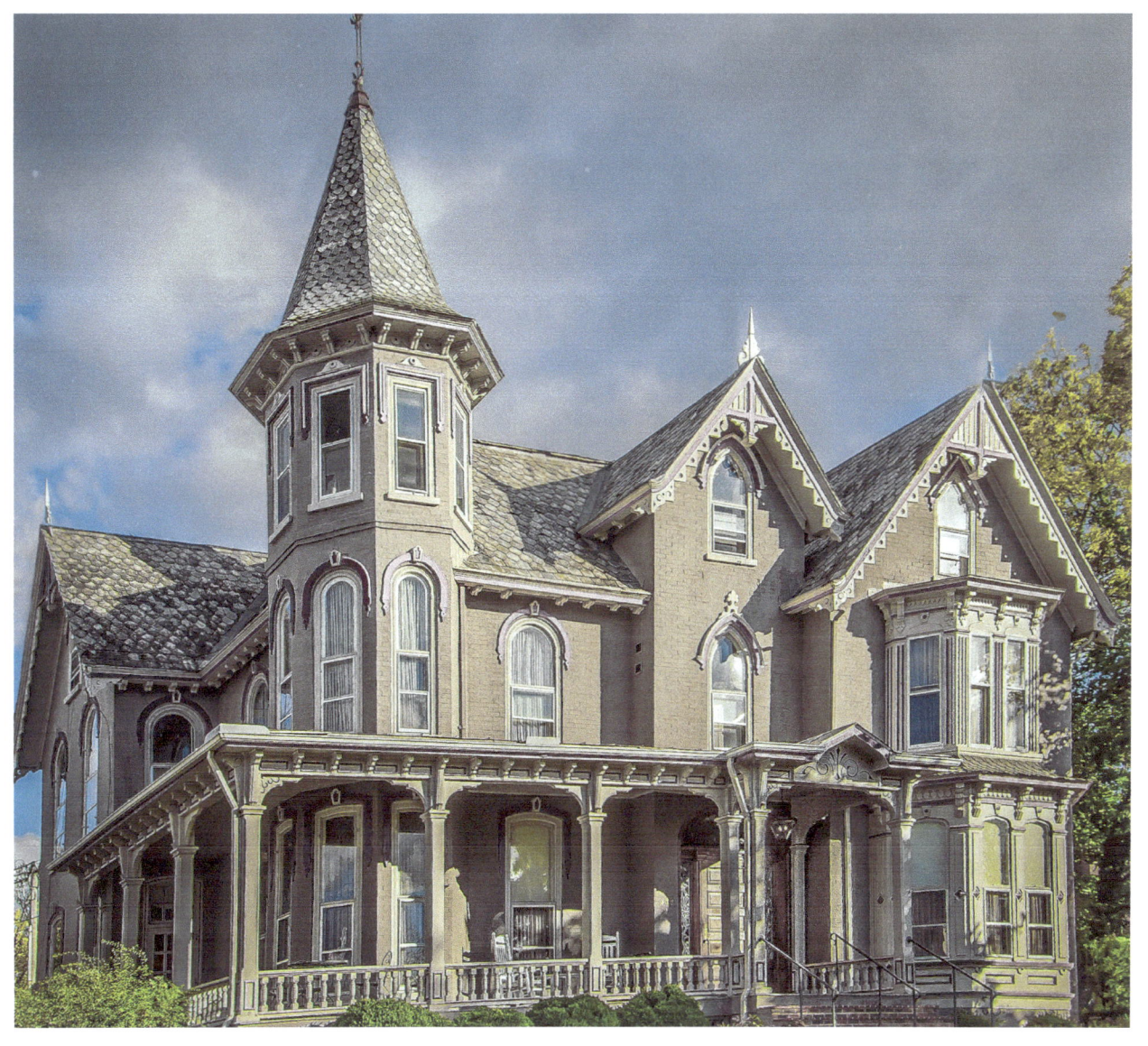

Joshua Wilton Restaurant & Inn in Harrisonburg, Virginia

Massanutten Regional Library in Harrisonburg, Virginia

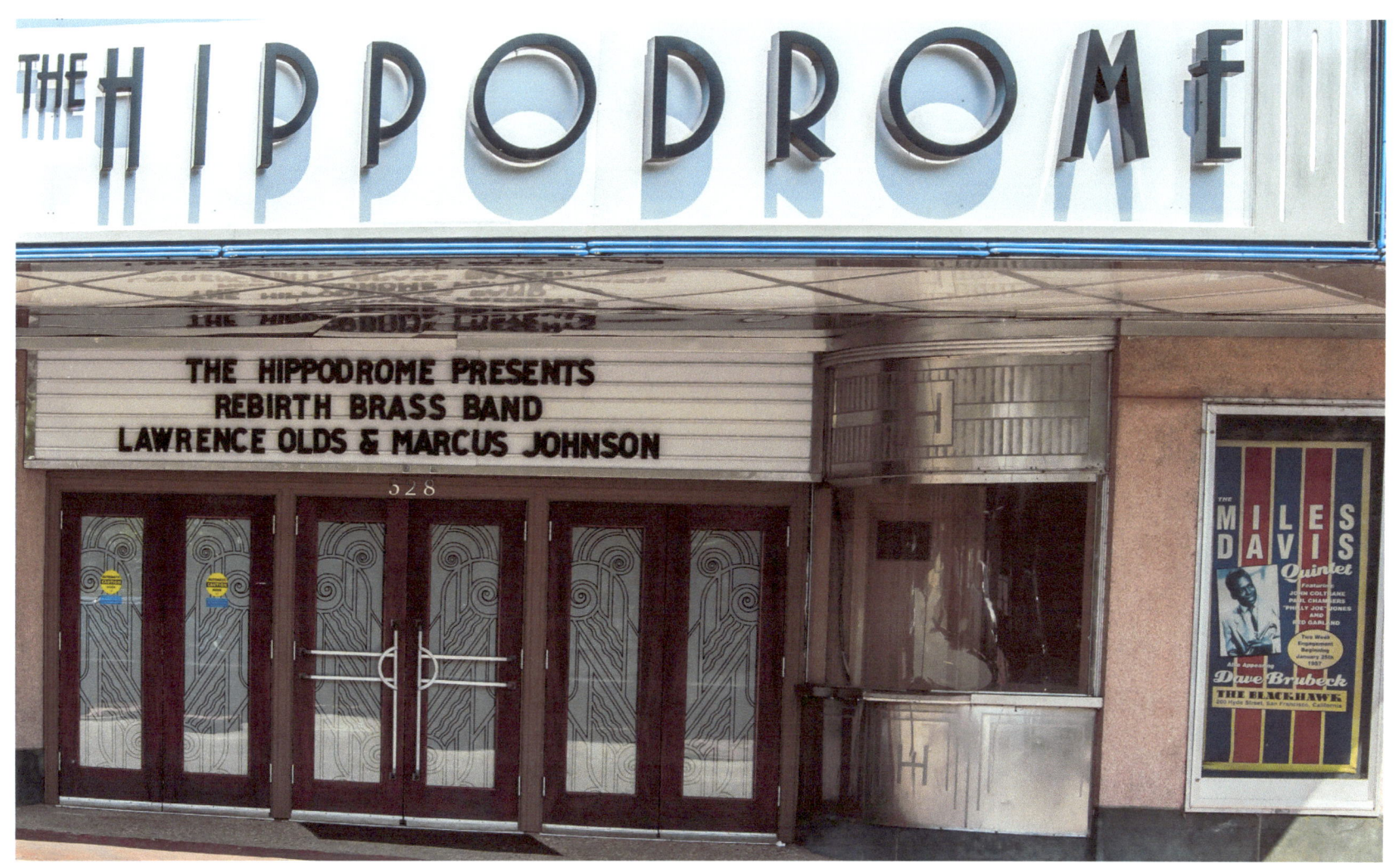

The Hippodrome in Richmond, Virginia

"Auto Sound Solutions," in Richmond, Virginia

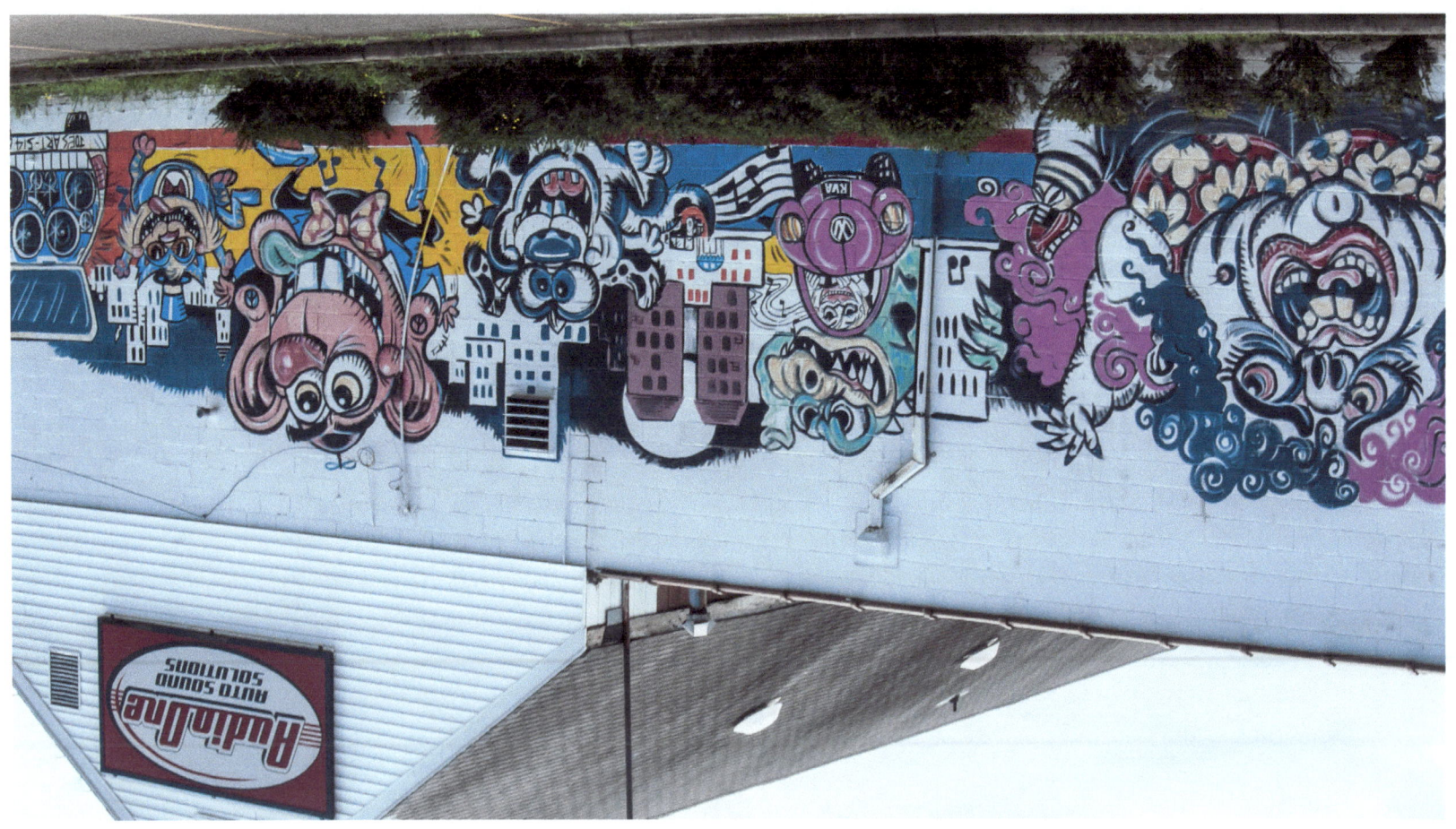

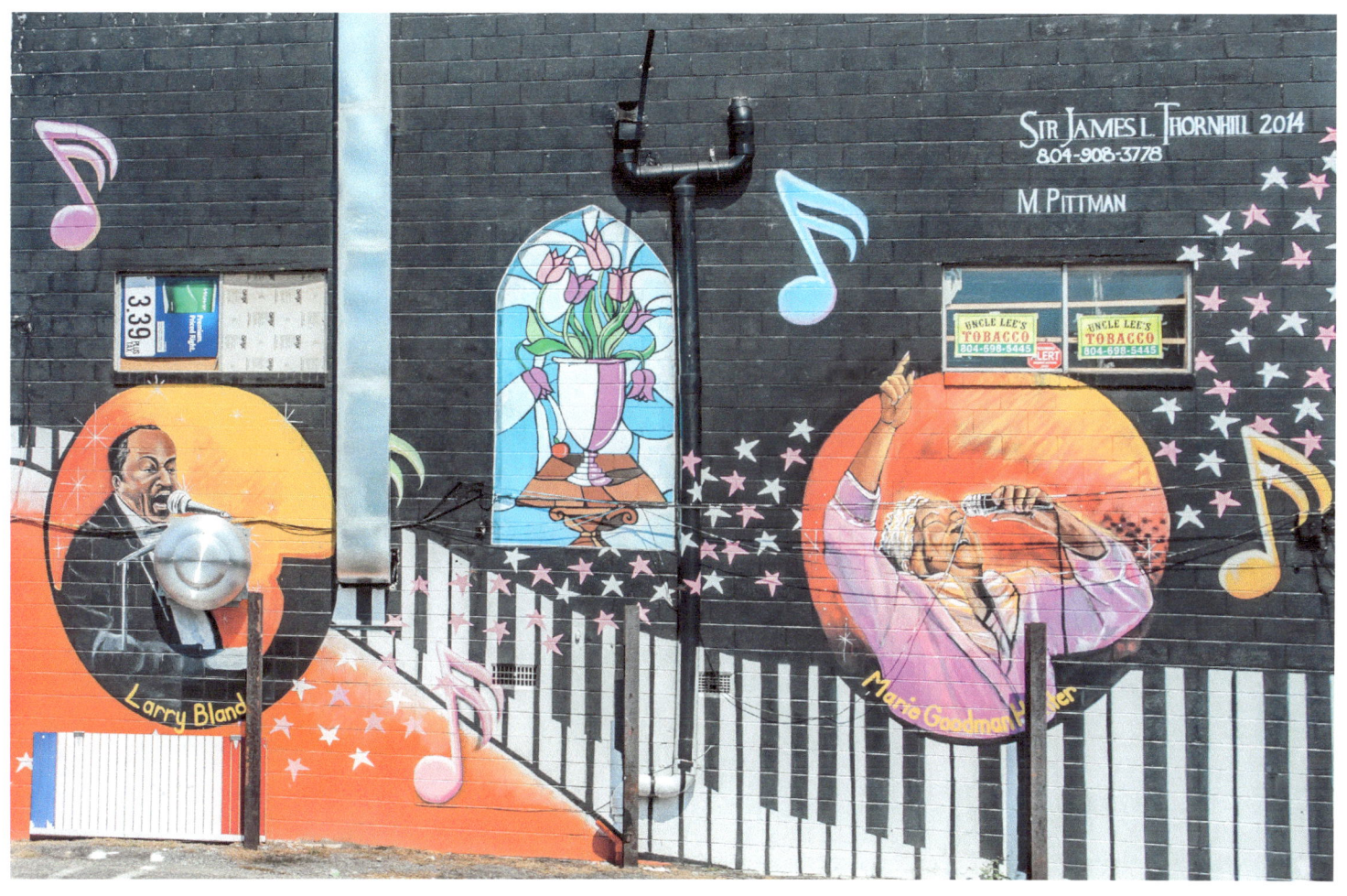

Mural of Musicians, Larry Bland and Marie Goodman-Hunter, of Richmond, Virginia

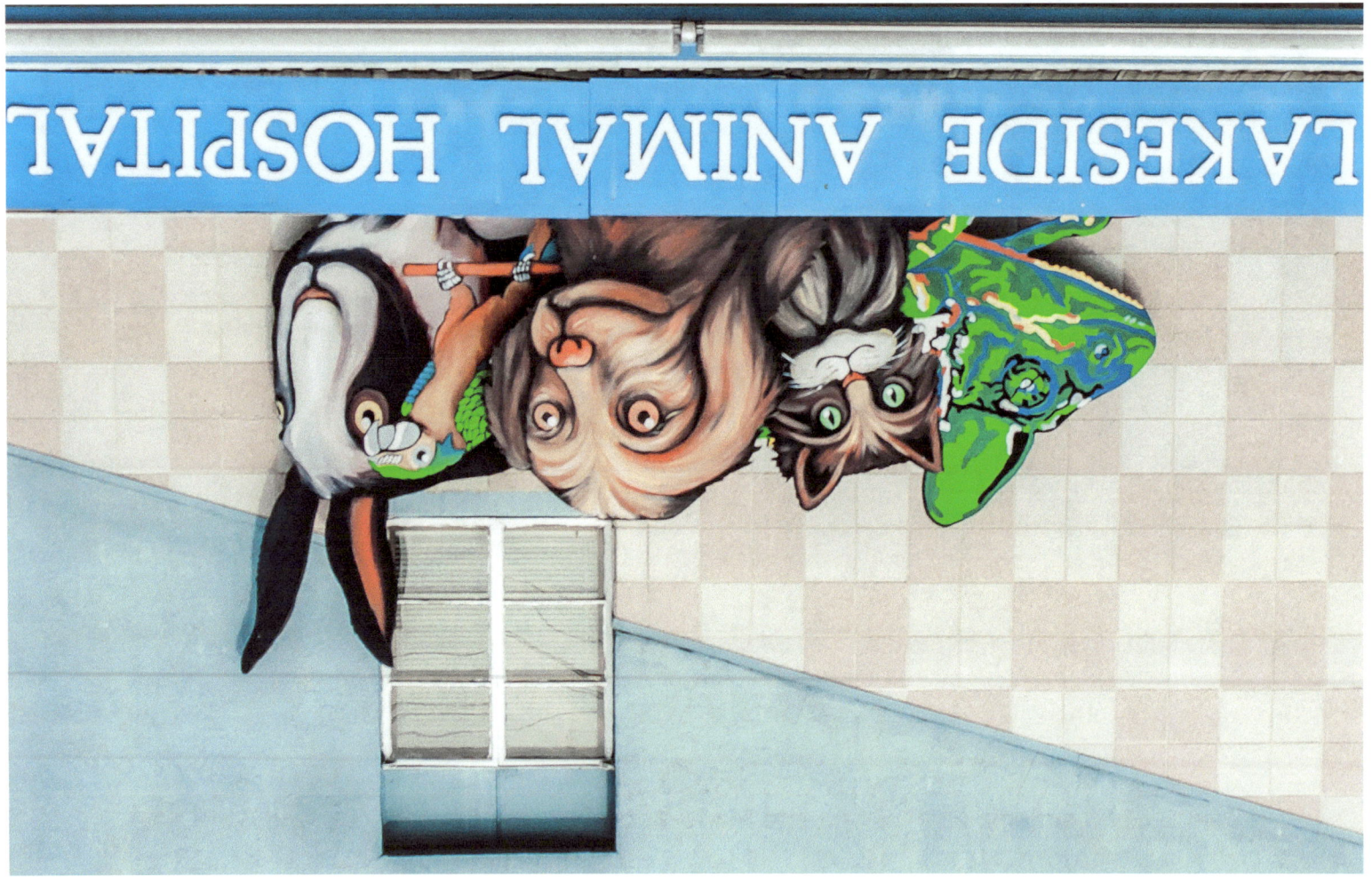

Pets' View at Lakeside Animal Hospital in Richmond, Virginia

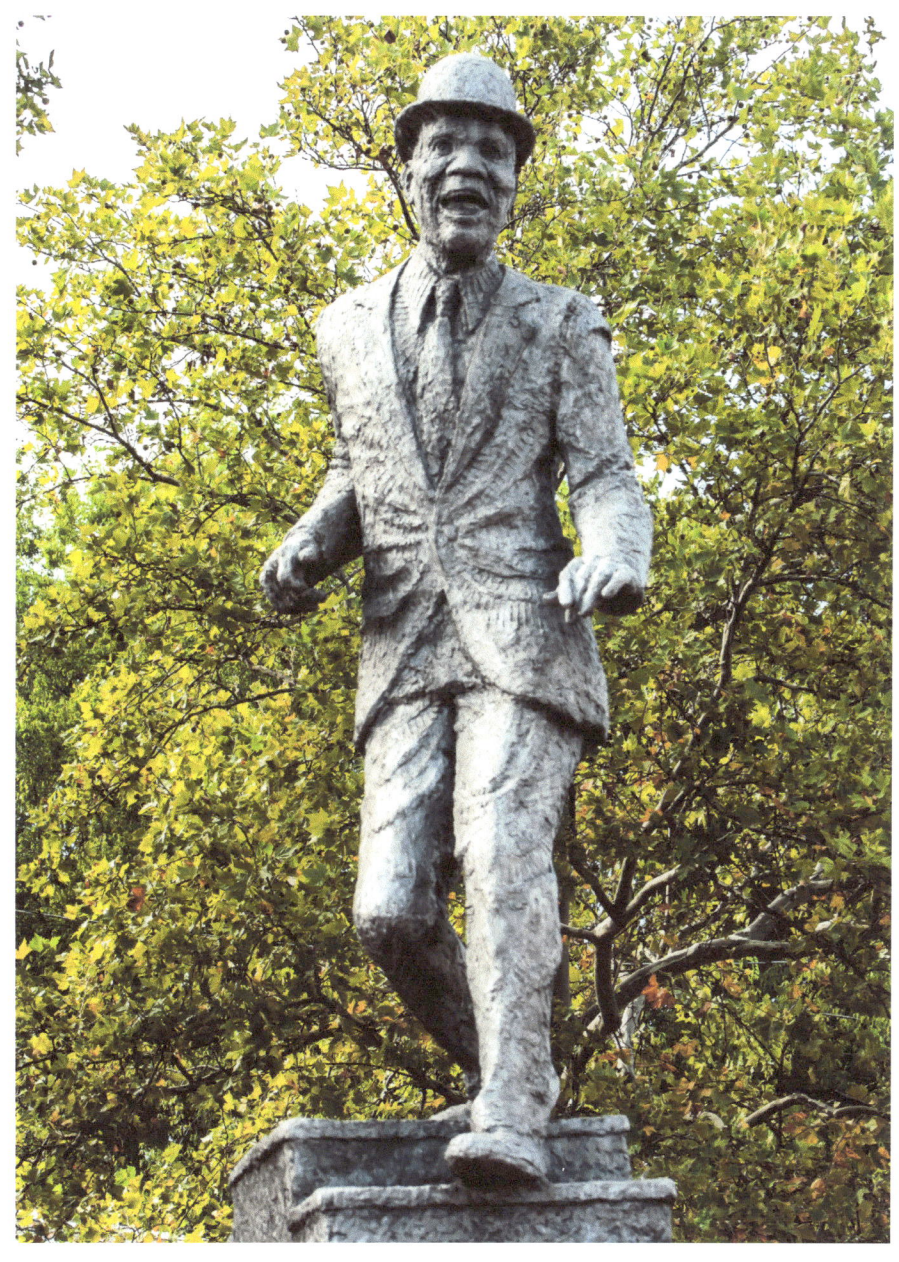

Monument of "Mr. Bojangles," Bill Robinson, American Dancer and Actor, from Richmond, Virginia

Index

Symbols

(1870) 21
1921 Dodge Brothers Touring Car 39
1927 Model T Speedster 38
1934 Ford Oren Firetruck 16, 17
1937 Studebaker Coupe Express 25
1941 Ford 9N Tractor Seat Pan & Steering Wheel
    27

A

Alpacas 1
Apple Country 41
Artful Vehicle 24
Arthur Robert Ashe, Jr. Monument 50, 51
Artistic Beauty 13
Artist's Impression 64
"Auto Sound Solutions" 68
"A View from Afar" 59

B

Barn Complex 42
Beauty of the Creek 56
Bill Robinson, American Dancer and Actor, 71
Black History Museum of Virginia 63
Black Wood-Framed Buggy 37
Buggy 18, 37

C

Campbell's Bridge 20
"Chicks Dig Vegetarians" 45
Christmastime 59
Clay Street Playground 58
Closely Parked Buggies 30
Colorful Buoys 61
Colorful Tower Silos 44
Crab House 60

D

Dayton, Virginia 18, 19, 27, 28, 44
Donkey 4, 5
Double Arch Bridge 56
Driving Wheel 26

E

Eastern Mennonite University 43
Eatery Sign 45
Equestrian 6
Ettrick, Virginia 20, 29

F

Firetruck 16, 17
Foxcroft School 42
Friends' Beach Home 46

G

Grazing in the Grass 1

H

Harrisonburg, Virginia iii, iv, 21, 43, 52, 56, 65
Hen 10, 11
Historic House 28, 29, 36
Historic Jackson Ward 62

J

James Madison University ii, 52
Joshua Wilton Restaurant & Inn 65

L

Lakeside Animal Hospital 70
Library iv, 66
Long Chapel at Zenda 21

M

Maggie L. Walker 46, 47
Massanutten Regional Library 60
Meems Bottom Covered Bridge ii, 31
Mennonites 33
Middleburg, Virginia 6, 35, 40, 57, 59
Monument 14, 47, 50, 51, 54, 55, 71
"Mr. Bojangles," 71
Mt. Jackson, Virginia 31
Musicians, Larry Bland and
    Marie Goodman-Hunter, 69
Mute Swan 2, 3

N

Norfolk Southern D9-40CW9313 26
Northern Shenandoah Valley 41

O

Observing Peacock 8
Original Railway Arches 20

P

Palomino Horse 7
Parked Horse-Driven Spring Wagon 32
Peacock 8, 9
Performing Horse 15
Petersburg, Virginia 36
Petersburg Waterfront on the Appomattox River
    (Civil War) 64
Pets' View 70
Picturesque View 19
Professional Tennis Player 51
Proposed United States National Slavery Museum in
    Fredericksburg, Virginia 40

Q

Quality of Life Image 49

R

Richmond, Virginia 46, 47, 50, 51, 53, 54, 55, 58, 62,
    63, 67, 68, 69, 70, 71
Rider's Dream 12
Rockingham County Turkey Capital 14
Ruins 20
"Rules the Roost" 11
Rumors of War 54, 55

S

Salamander Inn 57
Salamander Resort & Spa 6
Sandy Point, Virginia 48, 49, 60, 61
Spring Wagon 32
Statue of Door 58
Strasburg, Virginia 16, 17
"Struts Her Stuff" 10

T

Terrell Garage 34
Thanksgiving 57
The Hippodrome 67

U

Unionville, Virginia 34
Upperville Colt and Horse Show 15

V

Vintage Car Sofa Seat 22, 23
Virginia Union University ii, 53

W

Wandering Peacock 9
Waterfront View 48
Wayne's Home in Middleburg, Virginia 35
Welcoming Monument 14
Welcoming Pumpkin 57